Ask Ed:
Marijuana Law

DON'T GET BUSTED

Ed Rosenthal and William Logan, Atty.

Quick American Archives

Library of Congress Cataloging-in-Publication Data
Rosenthal, Ed.
    Ask Ed--marijuana law. Volume 1, Don't get busted / Ed
Rosenthal, William Logan. -- 1st ed.
    p. cm.
    Includes bibliographical references and index.
    ISBN 0-932551-36-X
    1. Marijuana--Law and legislation--United States--Criminal
provisions--Popular works.   2. Criminal procedure--United States
--Popular works.   3. Marijuana--United States.   I. Title.
II. Title: Don't get busted.
KF3891.M2R67 2000   345.73'0277
                                                     QB100-901343

00   01   02   03   04   5   4   3   2   1

Dedicated to legalizers who would make this book irrelevant.

"Got two reasons why I cry
away each lonely night
First one's named sweet Anne Marie
And she's my heart's delight
Second one is prison, baby
The sheriff's on my trail
And if he catches up with me
I'll spend my life in jail"

CONTENTS

Preface   vii

Introduction   ix

Chapter 1   **How the Police Bust People**   **1**

     A.   Informers   2
     B.   Accidents   8
     C.   Reducing Risk   17
     D.   Beat the Heat Guidelines   28
     E.   Police Investigation   29
     F.   DEA Operations   37
     G.   Rip-Offs   39

Chapter 2   **What to Do if the Cops Come**   **41**

     A.   Scenario 1: Cops Without a Warrant   42
     B.   Scenario 2: Cops With a Warrant   47
     C.   The Scope of the Search   47
     D.   Bail   48
     E.   Clean-up   50
     F.   Photos   51
     G.   Return of Seized Items   52
     H.   Right to Remain Silent   53
     I.   Arraignment and Preliminary Hearing   54
     J.   Forfeiture   56
     K.   Good Housekeeping   57

Chapter 3   **The Search**   **59**

     A.   General Information   60
     B.   Illegal Searches   60
     C.   Expectation of Privacy   61
     D.   Curtilage   62
     E.   Standing   63

Chapter 4 **The Arrest** **65**

    A. What Is an Arrest?   66
    B. Arrestees' Rights   67
    C. Questioning   68
    D. Detentions   68
    E. Post-Arrest   69
    F. Types of Charges   71
    G. Clearing the Record   72
    H. Who Makes the Arrest?   73

Chapter 5 **Choosing a Lawyer** **75**

    A. Lawyers' Licenses   76
    B. How to Choose a Lawyer   76
    C. Renter Beware   80
    D. Qualities of Good Defense Lawyers   82
    E. Do You Know Your Lawyer Yet?   82
    F. Retainers   84
    G. Fees   84
    H. Do You Need a Public Defender?   85
    I. Lawyer–Client Relationships   89

Chapter 6 **Medical Marijuana and the Law** **91**

    A. Current Legal Status   92
    B. Medical Necessity   95
    C. The Medical Referral Process   96
    D. Medical Registries   103
    E. Interacting with Police   104

Chapter 7 **Drug Testing** **107**

    A. The Rise of Workplace Drug Testing   108
    B. Workplace Testing Laws   110
    C. Types of Drug Tests   118
    D. Passing and Failing   127
    E. Recourse   134
    F. The Politics of Drug Testing   137

Appendix A: *Marijuana-Related Penalties:*
Federal & State-by-State **143**

Appendix B: *Federal Law* **159**

Appendix C: *Drug Policy and Law Resources* **171**

Appendix D: *Medical Marijuana Resources* **173**

Index **175**

AUTHORS

Preface, William Logan

Introduction, Ed Rosenthal

Chapter 1 *How the Police Bust People*

Katya Komisaruk – Section D
Ed Rosenthal – Sections A1 and E2
William Logan – Remainder

Chapter 2 *What to Do if the Cops Come*

Ed Rosenthal – Section A
William Logan – Remainder

Chapter 3 *The Search, William Logan*

Chapter 4 *The Arrest,* William Logan

Chapter 5 *Choosing a Lawyer*

Ed Rosenthal – Section C
William Logan – Remainder

Chapter 6 *Medical Marijuana and the Law*

Ed Rosenthal and Pete Brady

Chapter 7 *Drug Testing,* S. Newhart

Appendix A. Compiled by NORML
B. William Logan—Section C
Ed Rosenthal—Remainder
C. Compiled D. L. Church
D. Compiled D. L. Church

PREFACE

William Logan, Atty.

This book is about how to protect yourself so that you do not get into problems with the police or with the judicial system. It condenses the wisdom I have learned from legal cases, and many conversations with both growers and law enforcement over many years.

I have taken the essence of the lesson presented and tried to tell it as a story that you can understand, and hopefully benefit from. The form of the stories is not in any way representative of the intricacies of life or a particular legal situation. It would take a one-on-one discussion of your situation to do that.

This book should be used as a guide to avoid intersecting with the judicial system. It was designed to make you more knowledgeable about the laws and the moves, luck and karma of staying out of trouble. Knowing the rules may keep you safe from self-inflicted harms. Knowing the territory will help you stay safe, and if the cops do come to call, it can be a great relief to have a reference point by which to center yourself.

It is my belief that the modern user/grower/dealer is the karmic descendant of the great pioneers who made this country great. It takes resolve and tenacity to undertake a course of action that is thought by many to be foolish. Marijuana is still generally illegal in this country. Medical use laws are being passed in many states, and this seems to open the door to sanity, but the United States Supreme Court seems to be ready to shoot that idea down.

The decision to use pot and thereby break the law is intensely personal. That decision may affect your current freedom, the status of your criminal record for the rest of your life, and the freedom and wealth of your life partners (or even roommates). So many people smoke or grow marijuana, and always have, that it is apparent the process will not stop. The books and magazines with grow information are one side of this great exercise in individual freedom; this book on the law is another. Co-author Ed Rosenthal brings consummate expertise from the grow side of the table. He is the foremost authority on pot in the world. He taught me the basics of growing many moons ago. I used that basic training to defend a school-teacher accused of growing a million dollars of pot in her backyard. Her 13 plants were big, but not grown for anything but her own use. Proving that in the face of strong (but ignorant) prosecution gave me the first taste of the interweaving of law and marijuana. I've been hooked ever since.

Like sweet Linda, the vast majority of my clients are good people. They are not rapists, robbers, or thieves nearly as much as the general population. They generally pose no threat to the fabric of society by their decision to grow or use pot. This truly victimless "crime" hurts no one, except in the pocketbook, from high prices, and in the liberty book, from ignorant pernicious illegality. The most serious danger from pot is arrest. It is incomprehensible to me that the police will arrest a legal medical user, steal their medicine, take them to jail, and thereafter ignore the law and prosecute these poor souls. It happens every day in California, and across the nation. We have some state laws that try to protect the grower and smoker, but the vast majority of cops gladly break their oath to uphold all the laws.

While the laws against pot seem to be an immovable fixture of our crazed national conscious, many European nations are facing the reality of many years of scientific evidence that pot does no harm, and has great therapeutic value. These clear findings from every responsible scientific body that has undertaken to look at the issue without pressure from the U.S. DEA have been coupled with the equally clear message that people want to get high, and will pay for the pleasure. Marijuana tourism, from the Cannabis Cup to the head shops in Vancouver to the *piedmonte* of Switzerland, has proven to be a boon to local economies. These tourists are the most generally law abiding, gentle, and respectful of the bunch. They are the least ugly of the Americans that I have seen abroad. The choice of coffee and cannabis over alcohol as the mild intoxicants of choice has positive results in almost every situation. The businesspeople find these tourists easier to serve and please; plus other tourists like to do their thing without a loud drunk along. They spend a lot of money, and don't cause trouble. While in Amsterdam for several Cups, I did not see or hear of a single incident of a pot person running afoul of the law. Since there is no adjunct crime problem, and pot use is tolerated, there is no enforcement problem. Consequently it can be said that there is no drug problem with marijuana.

I look forward to the blessed day when we in America come to our collective senses and books like this are no longer necessary. Until then, good reading, Godspeed, and stay safe.

INDTRODUCTION

Ed Rosenthal

Since the U.S. government started in 1776 it has been engaged in war. In fact, there has not been a single day since that time, when the military has not been involved in some kind of "action." The list of countries it has been at war with includes Afghanistan, Argentina, Cambodia, Canada, Chile, China, Columbia, Cuba, Dominican Republic, England, France, Germany, the mighty empire of Grenada, Guatemala, Haiti, Iran, Iraq, Japan, Korea, Laos, Lebanon, Liberia, Libya, Mexico, Nicaragua, Panama, Philippines, Sierra Leone, Somalia, Sudan, Spain, Vietnam, and Yugoslavia. Not content with foreign enemies, the government chooses fights with its own people: first Native Americans, then Blacks, Mexican Americans, and other non-whites. But the U.S.'s longest running, most costly war is the War on Drugs.[1] It has claimed more casualties than any other war, and is widely regarded as a failure by most analysts.[2]

Everyone knows that there can't be a war against drugs. A kilo of marijuana cannot be arrested, arraigned, tried, and placed in prison. If it were, other prisoners would abuse it until it was all used up. The War on Drugs is really a war on people. If you are a drug user, grower, or dealer this is a war on YOU!

There are quite a few reasons for the War on Drugs, the anti-people war, and they all come down to money. Follow the money. The alcohol industry; the law enforcement, court, and prison systems and their war profiteers; pharmaceutical companies; drug testing and rehabilitation corporations; and finally their well-financed mouthpieces support the war—not for the good of society, but for their own pecuniary interests.

What does this have to do with you? The police want to make you a player in their 50-billion-dollar-a-year war games. And your role in the war, if the forces of ignorance have their way, is victim.

You could consider *Don't Get Busted* an antidote to the Drug War. It shows you a clear path through a territory filled with land mines. *Don't Get*

Busted can save you hassle, money, heartbreak, and perhaps years of diminished freedom.

Logan and I wrote *Don't Get Busted* to help you keep yourself free. It is extremely important that you read it and adapt its instructions to your lifestyle. No one can afford to get busted, or even worse, get convicted of a marijuana crime. It can literally ruin your life. Take advantage of our years of experience in and out of the courtroom and learn how you can avoid being suspect, and being targeted in the police scanner.

In nature, animals often use camouflage, confrontation, or flight to survive. Certainly confrontation and flight are not too effective when dealing with the police. *Don't Get Busted* helps to teach you the art of camouflage, of being invisible on the arrest scanner. It shows you what the police look for, how they look, and how to avoid appearing to be what they are looking for.

Don't Get Busted is not a dry tome that you promise yourself to read someday but which is too boring to ever actually start. It is written in down-to-earth style and shows many examples of do's and don'ts. You will learn something useful on every page. Just one piece of information could save you years of hassle. For this reason *Don't Get Busted* may be the most important book you will read this year.

How to Use Don't Get Busted

Everyone reading this knows someone who was busted in the last few years. This trauma leaves an indelible mark on the person for life. It's truly criminal that people are persecuted for such benign behavior, and shows that law enforcement—police, prosecutors, and the courts—have bloated budgets and unsocial policies and procedures. Unfortunately, this is the reality in which we live. Ignoring the risks increases the possibility of a bust, while adapting to the reality lowers the chances significantly. You owe it to yourself, and your family and friends to take a few simple steps to keep yourself out of jail.

Don't Get Busted should be read a few times so that you absorb most of the information and change your risk quotient. It will teach you your rights, how to exercise them, and provide you with common sense, easy-to-follow advice about lowering the chance of being busted. As you begin to use this information, your risk quotient will go down. You will be able to handle risky situations and smoothly extricate yourself from potential nightmares.

As I mentioned above, *Don't Get Busted* is a guidebook through the Drug War minefield. Reading it after you are in trouble will not be as effective. Instead, you should read this book before you have any problems. I know that's a difficult sell. No one likes to contemplate the downside because it's so negative, depressing and (let's admit it) frightening. There is so much "up" stuff to do and think about and this subject is a real drag. Yet there is reason to do so. Not being prepared to handle a difficult situation is rather frightening, too. Let's say there are sixty million marijuana users in the U.S. About 700,000 people are busted for it each year. That's about one point two percent. One percent doesn't seem like much—but one percent each year over a ten-year period increases that percentage to 12 percent, about one in nine people who use marijuana.

Actually, *Don't Get Busted* is not morbid. It's not so much about what to do after the bust as much as how to prevent it from taking place. Spending a few hours now absorbing the information in the book is insurance to prevent years of hassle. You will find answers to your questions, interesting stories, and lots of useful information that you never thought about. You will probably recommend it to a friend. Please do.

Random Thoughts

You're not paranoid—they really are after you. Although marijuana is widely accepted in society, it is not by the government, its police attack dogs, the courts, and politicians. Even though public opinion has changed, the government has resisted legal modifications. For instance, the police used to say, "We don't like these laws, we just have to enforce them." We know that was a lie. The police spokespeople have opposed reasonable changes in laws. Their unions have funded opposition to the recent marijuana initiatives. This is a bread and butter issue for them. No marijuana laws, fewer arrests, fewer cops. Don't become the jelly in the doughnut of a potbelly. Use the information *Don't Get Busted* provides.

I live in one of the few areas of the U.S. where marijuana law enforcement is not a top priority. Even so, I read about pot busts almost every day. Of course, most of these could have been prevented if the victims had only followed some of the simple advice offered in *Don't Get Busted*. The policies in much of the rest of the country as far as marijuana is concerned can be compared with the Taliban government of Afghanistan or the Iranian Mullahs. The continuous Reign of Terror called the War on Drugs is punctuated with jingoistic sound bites such as "Zero Tolerance," "Just Say No," and "Drug Free America." (Put down that coffee cup!—close Starbucks!—no more addiction maintenance centers.) Although it is a frightening thought, you must protect yourself. Please read this book so that you don't become another statistic in the government body count.

Better and Worse News

Public opinion is changing. In every election since 1996, U.S. voters have approved marijuana law reform every time they have been given a chance. Not too long from now politicians will finally get the picture. Then the jail doors will open and the victims will be freed. Perhaps there will be restitution to Drug War victims. Hopefully some of the Drug War terrorists will stand trial for "war crimes." Don't celebrate too soon. During this time of change these government-sanctioned thugs are especially angry that their free ride on the backs of marijuana users will soon be over.

As retribution for the increasing unpopularity of the Drug War, police are increasing pressure on marijuana users. There were more marijuana busts last year than ever before. It almost sounds like gray shades of the Indonesian militias in East Timor, who rampaged after the 1999 vote for independence. Be especially careful. Don't get caught by the thrashing tail of the dying dinosaur, which is the "War on Drugs." Please, for your own good, read and use this book. I wrote it for you.

---

1. GUESTIMATES—NO ONE KNOWS THE TRUE FIGURES, WHICH MAY BE MUCH HIGHER:
   - 9,500,000 people busted since 1985.
   - 700,000 people busted in 1999.
   - 2,000,000 people served time.
   - 450,000 serving time.
   - 60,000,000 parents, spouses, children, siblings affected by the trauma of a marijuana bust.
   - 1,000+ people killed as a result of marijuana law enforcement since 1985.
   - 0 people died as a result of simple marijuana use.

2. In 1937, when marijuana was criminalized federally, there were estimated to be 50,000 marijuana users. Using the criminal paradigm, the numbers of users increased to an estimated 60,000,000. This is an increase of 120,000 percent. In the last 15 years the addiction rate to tobacco fell by more than half without use of law enforcement forces and very few arrests, mostly through the use of education and civil regulation.

CHAPTER 1:

How the Police Bust People

A. Informers   **2**
   1. The Snitch Mentality   2
   2. Recognizing Snitches   3
   3. The Uninvolved Citizen Informant   5
   4. Undercover Cops   7

B. Accidents   **8**
   1. The Accident   8
   2. Loose Talk   9
   3. The Automobile   10
       a. A Clean Body   10
       b. A Clean Interior   11
       c. The Stash   11
       d. The Package in the Trunk   12
       e. Who Controls the Box?   14

C. Reducing Risk   **17**
   1. Suspicious Activity   17
   2. Respect Mother Nature   17
   3. Notes from Underground   21
   4. Photos   25
   5. Phone Taps   26
   6. Stealth   26

D. Beat the Heat Guidelines   **28**

E. Police Investigation   **29**
   1. Techniques   29
       a. Advanced Computer Sensing   30
       b. Cops: Smart or Stupid?   32
   2. Blessed Anonymity   32
   3. Sensitivity and Respect   34
   4. Record Keeping   36

F. DEA Operations   **37**
G. Rip-Offs   **39**

A. INFORMERS

Everyone who has read a whodunit or seen a detective movie has a good idea of how sleuths work. They examine all the evidence; they use tips, hunches, and psychology to find the perpetrator. Narcs use these techniques too. They also use lies, extortion, and blackmail to bust and convict people.

There are some things you can do to minimize contact with police, and to reduce the impact if such contact does occur. Most busts result from the information provided by an informer, from an accident, or from suspicious activity. Investigations also account for some busts. Many of them can be avoided with a little care and common sense.

1. The Snitch Mentality

People become snitches for a variety of reasons. Anger, self-righteousness, and envy are the three most common.

The number of people turned in by snitches for personal reasons pales in comparison to the number of people who are snitched on by arrestees who seek to reduce the number of counts for themselves. This is the cops' favorite way of busting people because it takes little time, effort, or intelligence on their part to get a good scorecard.

Charges are often reduced if a defendant "cooperates" by turning in

---

In one case, an attorney was charged with cultivation. He and his girlfriend had gotten into a verbal fight and he had ordered her out of his house. She dialed 911. When the police arrived, she said, "The marijuana plants are in the other room."

Another grower got into a disagreement with a customer, who called in the police.

One of two best friends, C, started growing. The other, D, couldn't because of his housing situation. At first C gave his friend D free pot. After a few months, he offered to sell stash to D at a nominal price. D became angry as C prospered. C was fronting D stash, but had not been paid. D asked for more pot. C refused and asked his friend to pay the money he owed. D turned C in.

A student in San Diego had 51 very small plants in his backyard. Unbeknownst to him, his neighbor could see the plants and, on the basis of his religious beliefs, condemned the use of God's herbs. He turned in his neighbor, and got a small financial reward too.

A group of workers were at a bar. A few of them went outside to smoke a joint. A coworker took note of who went outside and reported the stoners to his company because he resented working with "drug abusers."

A grower split up with his flaky partner and they divided the plants and equipment. Flake's plants died and he was very envious of his successful former partner, so he turned him in.

friends or associates. Under federal sentencing guidelines, and in state courts, a defendant's sentence is reduced if he or she turns in other people. These are potent weapons used by the state to induce people to snitch. They have caused family members and best friends to betray each other. These laws and policies have turned American morality on its head. Nobody respects a tattletale, yet American courts are turning citizens into snitches. Rather than teaching responsibility for one's actions, the government is now teaching its citizens that the honorable path is to unload your time onto someone else.

Obviously, smart people keep personal information and activities related to marijuana as secret as possible, sharing it only on a need-to-know basis. They avoid implicating themselves when illicit activities are discussed, and they do not show their garden to anyone, or even tell people that they own one. A good way to arouse suspicion is to "imply" such activities: Talking about them, including sounding very knowledgeable about how marijuana plants grow, or discussing how you used to deal, are sure to bring any inquiring minds closer.

2. Recognizing Snitches

How do you recognize a snitch?

Does someone you know seem not to need legal advice from a lawyer after a serious bust? Perhaps he is getting it from the cops or the prosecutor.

Does she want to talk about "old times"—including dates, names, and amounts—over the phone? Does he want to discuss where the money went? Does he suddenly begin to address friends by the names their mothers gave them, instead of "Smokehole" or "Stinky"?

Is there a big change in the drug-use habits of a recently busted friend? Did she really "reform" or did she agree with the cops not to use while she busted others? He always used to come and smoke a doobie. Now he just wants to score and split.

If the person who has sold ounces for years suddenly has a great deal on drugs, or offers to buy or sell them in quantities out of proportion to his or her usual amounts, or in partnership with a money or drug man who is "backing" the deal, something may be fishy.

Cops—and especially snitches—smoke and snort to "protect themselves" in an undercover situation. That can mess up their credibility in court. Generally they don't do it, and they almost always deny having done it, irrespective of the truth. The defendant's word against theirs is a dicey proposition at any time. If the defendant is saying he supplied and also did the drugs that the cops did, how does that help? How does he establish the cops' misbehavior without testifying to his own and blowing the rest of the case?

Before a prospective deal, the buyer might consider why a dealer who has the ability and desire to move a large quantity of product would give a small-timer such a good deal, or why such a dealer would even deal with him in the first place. After all, most people in the illegitimate business of dealing dope have all the connections they want or need. The middle ground of buyers who sell and sellers who broker for others is well filled.

Sometimes the cop or the informant buys small quantities several times, and then asks to do a bigger deal (buying or selling). Usually there is an unnamed person behind the scenes who wants to "okay the product" or "see your money" before the deal goes through. Police sometimes ask to see a sample, and then come back with a search warrant for the rest of it.

Remember the four elements of any drug bust: cops, crooks, drugs, and money. If cops and two of the other three are in the same room at the same time, there's trouble in paradise. All four together are really a problem.

> K was growing in the hills and lived in a house in the nearby town where he kept his equipment. He invited an underage girl over. She was later picked up for shoplifting and snitched on him in exchange for leniency.

> L was sentenced to 6 ½ years for cultivation. After 4 months in prison, he squealed to reduce his sentence by 18 months.

3. The Uninvolved Citizen Informant

The uninvolved citizen is considered the most reliable type of inform-ant. The police need no corroboration of his or her report of crime for them to act upon it. Usually the citizen informant is a person who is a victim of or a witness to a crime. Obviously, if someone sees a bank rob-bery and says, "That's the man," the police don't have to do much veri-fication in order to detain and probably arrest the suspect. The same holds if a hunter, fisherman, backpacker, or other tourist sees a back-country project, or if the meter man sees the Jesus Light beaming from under the garage door. Their information is probably good enough for the police to get a warrant and make a visit.

If somebody at the electric company notices that a meter is show-ing the consumption of a lot of juice, they may suspect the existence of a grow room and call the cops. They're sometimes rewarded with money for this tip ($1,000 per bust in my area), so assume they're looking diligently. This information may bring the cops to the house, where they'll try to see the project, or they may fly over with Forward-Looking Infrared Radar (FLIR) to see if it's hot. They check trash cans (perfectly legal), ask a compliant UPS for delivery records, and gather

> Grower E met two women in a bar in August and, later, the boyfriend of one of them. He offered to smoke a joint with them. The boyfriend was a former ripoff artist turned informer for profit.

> He figured this guy's leaf joint meant ownership of a garden. He "befriended" E and, a month later, after gaining E's confidence and inducing E to front him most of the harvested crop, turned him in.

information from cooperating grow-supply stores. All this goes into an affidavit to support a search warrant; it's usually issued, and the garden is usually busted.

Burglars and robbers sometimes become citizen informants. It might seem, on a moral and ethical basis, that the person who comes with larceny in his or her heart and a weapon on his or her hip is more deserving of prosecution than the person who is growing weed. It is

---

ASK ED #1
SNITCH Nov 98

We have a snitch in our town. What do you think we should do when he comes around my friends and myself?

T.,

Clair-Mel, FL

Refuse to have anything to do with the snitch. Tell him you don't want him coming around you, your house, children or friends. If he comes over to you or your group of friends in public, ask him to leave. If he doesn't, the group should re-assemble elsewhere without him. If he persists do not be violent, but you may have to be impolite. You may have to call the police and file charges against him as a stalker in order to get him to leave you alone.

Do not let him into your house, office or any space with a door which can be closed. A good line there is "Get your foot out of the door, you're not welcome here."

If he calls on the phone and says, "Hi This is Snitchy..." hang up, put him on "hold" or lay the receiver down. Don't talk to him even to say "Call me back later." or "How are you?" Don't let him hear your voice after you discover Snitchy is on the other end of the line.

Don't threaten him with violence, use violence or suggest that others use it.

Take solace knowing that snitches' actions have a way of catching up with them. They are like fish out of water, ostracized and isolated from their community. This makes it more difficult for them to thrive.

unusual, however, for police and district attorneys to be sympathetic to marijuana growers to any extent whatsoever. There was an almost-forgotten time when marijuana growers were given a reasonable disposition of the case (and, though rarely, a dismissal) in return for their testimony against the people who were there to rob them. This is no longer the case. The escalation of the drug war has made punishment more fierce and unforgiving than at any other time in U.S. history. Don't think that the police will have any sympathy for you under these circumstances.

4. Undercover Cops

Police and their agents don't have to admit they're cops if they're asked directly. Being undercover means you never have to say you're sorry. The whole modus operandi of undercover cops is to lie to you well enough to make you believe they're not what they are. Their lives may depend on their ability to fool you, an amateur. They seldom have much trouble. An average judge or jury member doesn't stand a chance of being able to tell when an undercover cop is lying. These guys are professional liars and they love doing it!

The mentality of the undercover cop is too strange for the average person to grasp. Why would someone be your friend, pay your bills, eat your food, stay in your house, occasionally sleep with you or your daughter (or son), and then bust you and everyone around you? I think these Judas-goat/informant/undercover narcs are sick people. The few honest ones I've met got out of the work as quickly as they could. Two years is about as long as anyone of real substance and moral character can successfully live the convoluted lies that the undercover lifestyle demands.

Statistics show that many narcotics enforcement officers are not honorable men and women. The rate of rip-offs, drug thefts, payoffs, and general sleaze in the drug law world is frightening. My clients don't all lie about the sleazy things cops or informants did to and with them, and if a tenth of what they say is true, then the system is in grave danger and we're living in a truly Orwellian situation. Who do you call if the cops are crooked? A hippie? The Guardian Angels? Parents Against Pot?

B . ACCIDENTS

1. The Accident

Accidents occur at the most inopportune times.

Although a person can't always stop accidents from happening, many of them can be prevented or ameliorated. For instance, a passive watering system is less likely to leak than an active one. Smoking a joint in a car while transporting grass could create a disaster. Using an unli-

---

ASK ED #2
TOP 10 STUPID GROWER TRICKS Dec 96

I thought I'd share this top 10 list with you.

10. Drive to the grow supply store in the car registered at the garden's home address.

9. Purchase all growing supplies by phone and have them sent to the garden address.

8. Tell two friends. They will be sure to tell two friends who will be sure to...

7. Invite everyone to the garden for "an after hours party."

6. Mess with your best friend's lover.

5. Mess with anyone if your lover finds out.

4. Plant a plot 2 blocks from the municipal airport.

3. Make yourself known by the local cops by speeding or other lame traffic violations, bar-room scenes or other nasty habits.

2. Smoke fatties when there's a major drought and you are the only one with reefer.

1. Talk about what a great grower you are and the great success of your last garden.

Pele,

Aloha, OR

Thanks for the list, Pele.

censed car, or one that stands out or has mechanical problems, is asking for trouble.

Grower G was growing in a commercial space above a gallery. The day before the gallery was to open a new show, the grow room sprang a leak. A rented car stalled and its trunk popped open while it was being towed.	There was a fire next door and the fire department broke in to reach the other apartment. Grower H bypassed the meter and circuit breaker to power his system. First there was a small fire, then the electric company investigated.

2. Loose Talk

Loose talk is a major category of being stupid in public. People don't talk to strangers about their medical or sexual problems. Using, dealing, and/or growing are at least that important! Telling anyone who doesn't need to know is taking a huge risk. Once you've told your secret, no one can predict or control who will hear it, what fact or fantasy they'll hear added to the repeated story, or where it will ultimately be told.

In small towns, everyone gets the local gossip: what you do for a living, who you sleep with, what habits you have. No one can control this, but you can be careful. It's necessary to have some "legitimate" work or source of income. You must be doing something to pass the time. Having inherited money is not uncommon, and removes the need to "work" for a living. Getting welfare assistance in the off-season and passing as wealthy when the crop comes in is not good form.

Conspicuous consumption in a small town may verge on public stupidity. Except for those who have a publicized inheritance, smart growers do not exceed reasonable expectations of visible income or lifestyle. Instead they go on vacation in the city, where $100 bills are commonplace, and where, without raising any eyebrows, they can be the people their neighbors never see.

If you party excessively at harvest time, and flash cash, you'll be identified as a grower. The garden's location will become a matter of speculation. If it is at or near your house, it will be found. If you attract the attention of the wrong sort of people, you and your family could be in serious danger. There are armed thieves out there who will kill.

Successful users, dealers, or growers resist the temptation to talk to strangers who seem to have an interest in marijuana. Even if the stranger doesn't know who you are, he or she can bring unwanted attention. Undercover cops often say they're growers, and seem to know a lot, and don't hesitate to talk about their projects. Smart growers, dealers or users won't take this as a sign that these are "real" or friendly people. Shouldn't these friendly people be more careful? Would you want to put your life in the hands of such fools?

People who act outrageous in public are often busted and cause official inquiries into their lives. This causes problems, especially if they're not prepared to answer questions about their money sources (the car, the land payment, and the food must come from somewhere).

| *One grower successfully harvested his crop, but got rowdy in the development where he lived.* | *The cops came, smelled the pot, and arrested him.* |

---

3. The Automobile

a. A Clean Body

The most obvious, and most often overlooked, cause of a bust is a vehicle that has mechanical defects. Broken lights, brakes, turn signals, taillights, headlights and even the lowly license plate light provide ironclad probable cause for any cop, anywhere, any time, to stop a vehicle. You must have a front license plate in many states. Make sure you comply with this law if it applies in your state.

After the stop, the vehicle is likely to be subjected to at least a cursory search. It could be more intensive. At worst, it's a thorough poke-around and smell, sometimes with a dog, looking for things "in plain sight."

To avoid suspicion and hassle, careful drivers also wash the car, clean the windows, and have a working horn and windshield wipers.

Some items in a car make cops less suspicious. A babyseat and some kids' items such as a doll, teddy, or book make cops less nervous. Legal papers, kept neat in a file box but clearly marked (not your case) makes them less inquisitive. Cars marked as company vehicles are less interesting to cops. A box of books in the backseat makes them more respectful.

The second major cause of mobile inconvenience is the traffic cop. Unless you obey all traffic laws, especially those small-town speed limits, you may have to talk with a cop. You should have your valid license and car registration with you. Even though some states don't require car insurance, many drivers have found it safest to carry it and have proof of it with them. Non-citizens should have a valid visa or green card ready.

It is a false economy to neglect basic car repair and maintenance. Not having the car in good and legal shape, or not having proper documentation can result in years in jail. The time you spend in preparation to protect yourself and your freedom pays off a thousandfold.

b. A Clean Interior

Keep the inside of your vehicle neat with as few items visible as possible. If there is nothing to search through, it is hard to conduct a search.

c. The Stash

A nosy cop can bust a suspect after seeing a roach or recognizing stash. If the suspect is carrying a stash of less than 1 ounce, perhaps an opaque container is enough to keep it private. Some non-see-through types of plastic kitchenware are popular in my area [or were until this book was published-Ed.], and stash boxes (especially road boxes) come in all types, sizes, and materials.

Less favored are containers that advertise or display their contents. I have a metal tin whose bold print announces that it contains "One Ounce of Grass" and also specifies "A LID OF GRASS." The original contents were tea bags of Lemon Grass Tea (a decidedly non-controlled substance). However, the canister begs for police inspection, and is far too cute for use outside the home. Clear plastic bags, or clear plastic wrapped packages are also bad choices because the contents can come into "plain view" much too easily.

One of the most ingenious road boxes I've seen is an oilcan or auto-products can that has been converted to a safe. These inexpensive, easily obtainable devices have saved many people a lot of trouble by being so obviously a "regular thing" that they were not even inspected. The cops know about these cans, so they might look into them. Some of them have reverse threads on the bottom; some have "real stuff" in part of the can, so that it sprays or pours a little of the advertised contents if tested.

If the police must open or, even better, if they must break open a package to see and recognize its contents, the law affords the victim of this break-in more protection from police intrusion and invasion of privacy. The stash package should be closed and sealed.

You should never consent to any search. However, you should not deny that the package is yours or disclaim any interest in it, because the law protects only those things that you choose to keep private. Of course, you must take some minimal, reasonable precautions so that a cop standing where he or she has a right to be (such as giving you a ticket or at a sobriety checkpoint) can't see or smell contraband.

Smart travelers don't smoke pot, use alcohol, or ingest any other drugs while they are driving. It's both illegal and stupid. People who can't control their habits are placing themselves in a more dangerous situation. They could suffer from their abuse of drugs.

d. The Package in the Trunk

If the police can't prove your fingerprints are on the inside of the container holding the pot, and you say nothing, the prosecutor and the cops must show somehow that you knew the dope was there. Possession of the container might not be enough to show you knew of the contents. Who put that in the car? When? Who else drives the car? All these questions, if left unanswered at the scene, can convince a jury that you're not guilty.

Larger packages are subject to the same rules. If the package is wrapped, sealed with tape, and not associated with the people in the vehicle (for instance, if it has been put in the trunk), the cops must have some evidence to show that people in the vehicle knew the package was there, and that they knew what was in it.

In one case, the packages were addressed ("That's not my handwriting!") to Joe Zingo, with Stan Smith's return address. At trial, the defendant has an open field run with the questions of who these people were, why they had the package, and what they were going to do with it. A courtesy extended to an acquaintance, such as taking the package to the post office, is not evidence that you committed a crime.

Let the police look for Joe and Stan, the owners of the package. Can the defendant describe them? Why must the defendant know where they live? How did she meet them and get their package? When will she see them again? A bit of mental preparation will enable you to answer the questions easily and consistently, at the proper time and place—which is not to the cops at the scene.

It amazes me that travelers rarely develop a cover story and rarely have lawyers and bail arranged. This lack of preparation looms much larger if they're arrested.

The single most important rule for travelers is to invoke their constitutional right to remain silent and to have a lawyer present while talking to the cops. In all cases, the traveler should be polite, identify himself, ask if he is under arrest ("Am I free to go?"), and refuse to consent to a search.

It may be that the cop stopped the person for a bad taillight, saw a wrapped and sealed box, and said, "What's in the box, kid?" or some local variation thereof. Ideally, the proper response is to politely ask, not answer, questions. This is an absolute right, and you should always protect your rights, because they protect you from unreasonable police intrusion into your life.

The perfect answer to the "What's in the box, kid?" question is to ignore it. Miss Manners says that difficult social situations are handled by politeness, so we don't have to be rude or lie to anyone. If we're asked a rude or indelicate question, ranging from "Can I search your car?" to "Are these kids yours or adopted?" the polite thing to do is not to answer the question, but rather to respond with a question of our own, which we follow up relentlessly until the original question is forgotten or abandoned.

A good response to the "What's in the box, kid?" question is to ask why you were stopped, or to offer the paperwork to the cop while talking about the license, the car registration, the weather, or your cousin Bill. Given the physical distractions of handling the papers and listening to your ramblings, the questions may fade.

If the cop persists in his inquiry as to whose package that is, what's in it, and why it's in the car, you should ask him why he wants to know, what the problem is, what he thinks it is. Does he have a tip, or is he just curious, or what? If it's just idle curiosity, he has no need to know. You need no reason whatsoever to say "No" to cops who just want to poke their noses where they shouldn't be. Just be careful to be polite to them.

The cops may say that a suspect's refusal of consent to search can be used as evidence of guilt and of knowledge of what the suspect (and now the cop) knows is in the box. That's a lie. Assertion of constitutional rights can never be held to be evidence of guilt of anything. If that weren't the rule, we'd be forced to choose between the rights guaranteed to us, and suffer for making the choice.

If you don't consent to a search of the box, and don't say it's not yours, there are very few legal ways a cop can get inside the box, and almost all of them require a search warrant issued by a judge. If you haven't done anything else to get yourself arrested, the judge won't issue a search warrant based on your refusal to consent to a search, and unless the cop lies and says you consented to the search, the evidence will be suppressed.

e.   Who Controls the Box?

There's no harm in saying that the box is in your custody and under your control. This is not admitting any knowledge of its contents.

If you say the box is not yours, you'll later find that you goofed. The law protects only owners and others with a legitimate expectation of privacy in an area searched or a thing seized. If the box is not yours and you don't assert the natural, logical right to control it and exclude others, you don't have legal standing (discussed below) to suppress any evidence uncovered by the search.

People usually deny ownership because they feel that asserting some association or control over a package with drugs in it will incriminate them. "Hey, man, it ain't my package," in all its more or less eloquent forms, regularly appears in police reports. If the box is in the car you're in, whether it's yours or not, the jury will want to hear some explanation of the W's—Who, What, When, Where, Why. The time to give that explanation is at trial, not at the scene. Absent some other explanation, the jury normally believes that people own items found in their cars.

When the subject of a stop tells the police that the box is in his custody and under his control, he is not necessarily admitting that he knows the circumstances surrounding the contents. He must be able to explain coherently how he got the box, from whom, and what his intent was with regard to it (apart from the contents, of which he has no knowledge).

If you give an entangled explanation, the cops will immediately begin to try to discredit the story. You are better off waiting for the attorney before giving a detailed statement.

If you take someone else's package to the store or post office for her, you have the possessory right to control the box, and to keep other people from taking it or opening it. If you say, "The box is in my custody [or control] now and I cannot give you permission to open it," you've

---

Grower I lived in a suburb in South Dakota. Other houses in the tract had crew-cut lawns and looked neat. I's house had a lawn overgrown with weeds and messy drapes showed through the windows. J lived in a quiet apartment development, most of whose tenants were young families. There was constant traffic to and from his apartment. Both of these people stood out, which made them suspect.

🌼

M was an oil maker. One spring day, he went to his town's fair, where he got into a conversation with a narc who was in uniform that day. The cop told me later that he smelled pot on M. Several weeks later, M went to City Hall to apply for a permit. The same cop noticed him and, obviously, learned his name and address. Later that day, while M was out, a 911 hang-up call was mysteriously made from his house. The same police officer answered the call and found some oil.

asserted enough of your rights to challenge the search later, and you can still go to trial saying "Prove it!" about the contents of the box.

If you say you have control over the box, this doesn't mean you know what's in it, or have any possessory or ownership (or even use) rights in the contents. Opening a package prepared and ready for mailing, without a warrant, is a fairly serious thing. On the other hand, mailing drugs is a major crime.

If things are sticky, you won't talk yourself out of an arrest. The cop will just take your statements and twist them or remember the bad parts. If you say nothing, there will be no debate about what was or was not said. Any statement that helps will help more with a lawyer present. Any statement given without a lawyer will be used to screw you later.

It is a truly rare person who is adequately prepared and able to tell the story to the cops at the scene and to have it told to his or her benefit later in court.

ASK ED #3
STEALING POWER Aug 97

I have 200 ft.² growing under a combination of two metal halide (MH) and four high pressure sodium (HPS) lamps. My electric bill shows that I use about 3,000 kilowatts monthly. My garden is located in an industrial area, so the power useage is not unusual. However, my electric bill comes to almost $500 a month.

A friend told me that he could re-arrange my electric for about $1500 so that about two thirds of the electric would be drawn around the meter, indicating less power consumption and lowering my bill. He said that he could save me over $300 a month.

Should I do this?

Maquelle,

San Francisco, CA

Messing with the electric meter is a stupid idea for several reasons. First the ethics of it. Stealing electricity is theft. Even though your power company (Pacific Gas and Electric) is insensitive to the public good (as in their insistence on building nuclear plants) and

C. REDUCING RISK

Here are some simple ways you can reduce your risk.

1. Suspicious Activity

The United States is the most violent industrialized country. As a result, it has one of the most paranoid populations in the world. Americans are suspicious of people who simply look or act differently than they do. This has serious implications for people who are connected with marijuana.

2. Respect Mother Nature

Disrespect for Mother Nature can invite a bust. I've visited gardens where the ground was littered with trash—discarded grow supplies, empty fertilizer boxes, broken pipe fittings, and other junk.

---

has very high rates for their energy, stealing power from them is still theft and not high moral ground.

Secondly, the savings are not worth the possible cost. Your electric costs you a total of $6,000 a year. If your "friend" jumped the meter, you would save $4,000 a year. Figuring your harvest conservatively, each light produces a pound every three months, so the garden yields 24 pounds a year, and has a value of about $100,000. Your electric is only six percent of revenue. With tampering it would come to two percent. Does it pay to put yourself in jeopardy for a savings of $4,000 a year on a net profit of at least $70,000?

The third reason is that lowering the electric usage might arouse some suspicion by the electric company, which likes to see steady patterns.

If you hate the high electric rates, which in your area are paying for the inefficient nuclear power plants PG & E insisted on building, contribute some of those profits to one of the utility rate consumer groups such as TURN (Towards Utility Rate Normalization), Tel. 415-929-8876, which fights for consumers against rip-offs by the utility companies.

A friend who read this said, "It's like skimming from the mob—not profitable for long."

ASK ED #4
LEAF TATTOO Feb 95

I am considering having a leaf tattooed on my shoulder. I have no other tattoos but I feel a small leaf would signify my relationship with marijuana.

My wife feels that the tattoo would be a threat if seen by the police or other government officials. I've never had hassles with the police.

Obviously it's not wise to advertise that you are involved with an illegal activity, but don't I have the right to wear a leaf or any other symbol of freedom without the fear of being harassed by law enforcement?

What would you do in this situation?

Armman Leafless,

Minneapolis, MN

Listen to your wife. With a leaf tattoo you may be conspicuous when you do not wish to be so. Bob Dylan wrote, "Don't follow leaders, watch the parking meters." I interpret this to mean, Stay inconspicuous. He also said, "To live outside the law you must be honest." From modern experience I say, "To live outside the law you must be careful."

The tattoo could be embarrassing or worse if seen at an inappropriate time or by an inappropriate person. Remember, most busts not instigated by informers are accidental. The body decoration increases the accidental factor and perhaps the informer percentages.

You do have other choices. They include:

Temporary leaf tattoos—Easy on and off. You could wear one on your forehead at the demonstration Sunday and show up clean for your job as bank vice-president Monday.

Wearing marijuana—T-shirts, shorts, hats, belt buckles, wallets and other personal items. These can be as private or public as you wish and can be changed with a couple of overhead motions or quick pocket insertion.

Join and participate—Get active in legalization work either alone or as a member of a group. This really shows your commitment to the leaf.

In one case, the forest itself seemed to be offended and an eerie sequence of events "accidentally" led to the bust. Trash carried out by the growers, and small animals who raided it, were spotted quite far away, arousing curiosity. An observer took a short walk to a nearby ridge overlooking it all and made a call to the cops, who easily followed the trash dispersal pattern and located the garden and the growers. The man who called the cops said he could see the litter, not the plants; in the remote back country, that was enough to bring it all down.

One successful grower always left her shoes at the garden and took care not to leave tracks as she came and went. She knew immediately when a person had been on her path, but by carefully following the tracks, she was able to tell the project had not been compromised. She was brave, and took many extra precautions until harvest.

Cut branches and uprooted vegetation are a giveaway. Smart growers treat the garden as a part of the natural landscape. The aerial over-flight has ended the clean-cut methods of the 1970s. The cut end of a branch may stand out because its color or shape is not natural looking. A 3-inch-diameter branch cut can be visible for a quarter mile. It is easily, if accidentally, spotted from any airplane or helicopter that happens by, cops or not.

Any disruption of nature stands out. Non-natural shapes and colors stand out dramatically. From an airplane, the circular shape of the

One project was compromised by the removal of one limb of a tree. The people on the main path had never considered fighting their way through the live oak brush covering a well-constructed and almost invisible path. The location was blown after four years because one of the laborers decided to make it easier to get to the garden. He removed one branch. The path stood out and begged to be walked on. It led to the water spring and the garden site. No bust, but only because the grower immediately knew it was over and moved the garden.

piled brush enclosure, or of the Doughboy pool used for water storage, is eye-catching.

Paths are also quite noticeable from the air; if they lead to anything of interest, a bust will follow. Established animal trails to and from gardens are often used. Obvious paths, from anywhere people might be expected to come from, should be avoided. Rocks can be used as stepping stones, tree limbs as bridges; other "trailless trails" can be devised to break the line from any well-traveled path to the private one.

Unbusted growers' paths are tended like Zen gardens. A person who "sees" the environment can "read" which creatures have been visiting. There are usually areas of clean, bare dirt where one would ordinarily leave a trail. To conceal activity, these are swept clean coming and going, leaving no tracks to be seen.

ASK ED #5
THE 400 WATT BILL Aug 99

I was wondering how much would a 400 watt HPS system affect my electrical bill, and if it would be noticeable to authorities. I live in a two bedroom apartment on the ground floor of an apartment complex.

Luscious,

Internet

I am about to start a garden under 400 watts of HID light. I am concerned about being detected. I know The National Guard sweeps areas with infrared to look for grow rooms. My grow room will only be a couple of plants, will this be a problem?

Young V.
Clarksburg, WV

I don't know the electric rates in your area so I can't give you an estimate of the addition to your bill, but I can tell you how much additional current you will draw. You are using a 400-watt lamp and probably some fans and controllers. Let's say the total electric draw is 500 watts, ½ kilowatt. When the system is on 24 hours a

3. Notes from Underground

Almost everyone knows that a clearing in the woods with neat rows of plants in it is easily spotted during a flyover or a walk-by. Any investigator who saw something so obviously the work of human hands, in such a remote area, would instantly be suspicious.

Fences erected to keep deer or cows out of the patch can disturb the landscape sufficiently to appear from the air as geometric and regular—not natural—features. Another argument against fencing is that any person who happens by knows that something is going on behind the fence. Cops in airplanes and helicopters look for the color and shape of the plants and the shapes of garden areas.

day during vegetative growth, the total daily use will be 12 kilowatts. During flowering, when the lights are off 12 hours a day, the total will be half that amount, 6 kilowatts. In a 30-day month, the vegetative cycle would use 360 watts and the flowering, 180.

I recently visited a well-lit, medium-sized office (11' x 16') that was lit by 10 4' 40-watt fluorescent tubes. 4 100-watt incandescent bulbs use just a little more than 400 watts. 400 watts of electricity to light a room is not suspicious.

Electrical rates vary between 7 and 15 cents per kilowatt. At 10 cents a watt the additional electricity will cost $36 a month during the vegetative cycle, and $18 during flowering. I don't think that this increase will ring a bell at the police station.

As long as the garden is not near an outside wall, there is virtually no chance of it being picked up as suspicious. Gardens in closets, basements, or rooms using only 400 watts of light do not heat up the room enough to create a significant change in heat pattern at the outside surface of the space being photographed.

The infrared detector measures the relative heat at the surface being photographed. It cannot recreate a picture of a room. The detectors work only during the night since too much solar radiation interferes with their operation. A flower room on during the day and off at night would not emit heat at times that the infrared is effective.

There is some truth in the idea that marijuana has a particular color. Some studies show that a particular wavelength of light is specific to marijuana plants. The Feds have used super-sophisticated, computer-controlled, color-differentiated spectroscopic analysis from satellites and spy planes to determine the extent of coca and cannabis cultivation worldwide. The usual "color bust" comes because the plants are well fed and well watered, unlike the struggling native vegetation. One grower's solution was dinner for all the plants in the neighborhood. Another's was a foliar spray of inert color.

In a number of cases, I've gone up in a small plane, checking to see whether cops actually could have seen the garden as they said they had. The bottom line, most of the time, is that the judge agrees with the cops that they saw what they said they saw. It's very difficult to prove they didn't see what was, in fact, there. In my experience, cops can identify cannabis from 400 yards.

Water lines are responsible for some seizures. If the line is not buried at least 6 inches deep, it has a very distinctive infrared signature (worm lines on the hillside), easily identified by the cop with an infrared video camera. If a hiker or deer hunter sees water lines or an in-stream pickup system, either a bust or a rip-off may soon follow. A garden using a stationary reservoir as a water source is an easy bust. One grower claimed he was never busted because he used a water-bag reservoir, mounted in his pickup, to irrigate his plants.

Paths to and from the water and the project are clearly visible from the air, and often direct attention to the garden. It is likely that animals have made trails near the project. These trails can be used gently, but not cut and pruned and worn down to a wide swath.

Careful growers want to know before they get to the project if someone has been there. One grower told me she developed several spots along the path where she could check for strange footprints. She found that both sandy and muddy areas can serve this purpose. Native Americans used tall grass. They could see where it had been trampled.

Likewise, footprints (shoe tracks) are just like fingerprints. Wise growers avoid taking home the shoes they wear in the garden. Even a particular kind of mud found on shoes, or particular vegetation stuck to clothing, can be used in court.

Usually man-made things, not the plants themselves, attract attention. I've gone into the bush with cops and fishermen and stood 10 feet from a garden, expecting someone to notice and comment. They didn't see it, I didn't mention it, and we walked away. I took a picture in Jamaica when our tour bus stopped so we could enjoy the scenery. Only later did I see the 50 or so 8-foot-tall marijuana plants about 30 feet from the bus.

Good fences around the property, posted with lots of "No Trespassing" signs, can help—or can hurt if they stick out as an overly emphatic assertion of privacy.

Growers are sometimes trapped by their tools. Cops try to match equipment from the project with material from the house. If the grower has garden tools at home, do they match those at the garden? Did she buy the pump they found? Are the suspect's fingerprints on the hoses, timers, books, food, and other items at the site? Most growers leave prints around because it's almost impossible to work on a garden and always wear gloves.

The smart grower keeps her stash well hidden. She expects that if cops bust a garden and connect it to her, the cops will search her house and sift through her life history.

Paper trails of money and drug sales are hard to hide and easy for the cops to get. The prophet Bob Dylan said, "To live outside the law you must be honest." Or at least appear so, say I.

Someone else might put a different spin on a person's irresistible urge to save every roach and empty bag. The prosecution could claim that it is "prepackaged marijuana for sale" and "packaging material."

Violence in the trade has increased as the per-ounce price of marijuana has rocketed past the per-ounce value of gold. If a small bag or a plant is worth thousands of dollars, there are reasons to be fearful as well as careful. However, guns always imply violence, and the cops and courts take them very seriously. The cops and the system consider any gun or other weapon a big threat. People face years in prison for having

ASK ED #6
DEVELOPING PRINTS Nov 94

Dear Ed,

How should I go about getting my pictures developed?

Bud Man,

Rialto, CA

PHOTO ADVICE March 97

I would like to take some pictures of my crop. Would I be risking a bust by having my film developed at a local drug store or super-market?

Gat-Man,

Daytona Beach, FL

It would be safest not to have the film processed locally before the garden was harvested, dried and safely stored. It would probably be best to take it to the most impersonal places, especially where the processing is done off premises and is just picked up from a clerk who has never had a possibility of seeing the images. Another possibility is to take them to a fast (same day service) photo developer in a large city with a walk-up window. For the most paranoid, or perhaps really the most careful there are further precautions to take. Go to an adjacent town. Park the car away from the mall and walk to the store. Go to a place that does a lot of business and don't stand out, either with clothing or conversation. Pay in cash. Pick up the photos promptly.

Personally, I use two different services. One is a locally owned and operated quick photo place located on the commercial street of my residential district. He obviously sees the images but has never said a thing to me about the subject matter. I also use a mail-order photo developer and printer that provides services unavailable locally. The mail-order company has always treated my jobs professionally and once again, the subject matter is treated routinely. I have never had a problem with either photo service.

a gun available for offensive or defensive use when growing or dealing marijuana. *I advise all growers to get rid of their guns.*

4. Photos

Many people photograph gardens they've worked on. Some photos may be from this year or last year; some might be from 10 or 20 years ago. Photos are very strong evidence against you. Inventive federal prosecutors have seen CCE (Continuing Criminal Enterprise) charges lurking in a proud grower's photographs.

Occasionally the photo processor is the rat. The lab technician may look at your roll of film to pass the time or for quality control. If she notices a garden, she may report the photos. Rewards are regularly given for information that leads to a bust, especially one with a property seizure attached to it.

INCRIMINATING PHOTOS Aug 95

I have lots of pictures of both inside and outside plants that I grew. Is it possible to get busted because of those pictures?

Concerned Rob,

Ogdensburg, NY

Anyone having photos developed should be very careful about where they are taken for processing. People have been harassed or arrested because of the acts of self-righteous employees or proprietors.

It is not illegal to possess the photos. However, after a bust the prosecutor might use the photos as evidence of the crime or of a continuing crime. If a person showed the photos to another, and explained that he had grown the plants depicted, that would be enough to at least start an investigation.

The photos should be stored in a place which is not likely to be connected to a garden. That way they cannot be seized and used as evidence.

5. Phone Taps

After a bust (or even before), outlaws sometimes notice clicks and pops and wheezes on the phone line. Is somebody listening in on your conversations, or is it just a flaw in the phone company's service? The technology available to any major law enforcement group enables it to tap phones without your being able to tell. They merely have to put something near the wires that eventually lead into your house in order to pick up what's going over those wires.

On the other hand, it's extremely difficult to obtain a legal wiretap warrant. Usually a federal judge must review the circumstances and issue that warrant. These warrants are usually issued only in the largest, most involved drug investigations. The decision as to what constitutes a "big" drug dealer or investigation is entirely dependent on how much the cops have to do and who else they're hassling this week.

A final observation: Very few policemen would be willing to risk their careers by conducting an illegal wiretap. If one were discovered, it would cost the cop not only the case but probably also his job and pension, and might even lead to prosecution and a prison sentence. Most police officers are too concerned about their own welfare to commit this violation of the law.

Car phones, or any other cordless instruments, have no privacy. The cops can, and do, listen to the radio waves legally without a warrant. A simple scanner allows anyone to listen. There are so few exceptions to this fact that smart dealers take this slogan as gospel: "Use a cordless, go to jail."

6. Stealth

Careful growers remove nails and strings used for drying racks after use. All leaf parts, stems, pots, and equipment are removed and disposed of.

All unused growing supplies are placed in or near the vegetable garden, or off the property. Supplies such as manure, hoses, or anything like that are not stockpiled.

Starter plants in a greenhouse are an invitation to trouble when seen by a neighbor kid poking around the yard.

Cop photos showed a 30-bag stash of worm casting, a soil supplement, next to a shack in the woods with no landscaping. It was visible from the front driveway of the house, a place where the cops have an arguable right to be, even on pretty slim grounds.

I am repeatedly amazed by the number of otherwise sensible growers who think nobody notices what he or she is doing.

The United States Supreme Court says you can have no expectations of privacy for trash you place in a can and put out for collection. That means the cops can root around in your trash like true pigs and become amateur garbologists. This esoteric science is used to generate expert (?) opinions about what is going on inside the house, based on what is thrown out. It shows that there is probably no depth to which the cops will not descend in order to bust you for growing. They'll arrange with your trash collectors to receive the trash picked up by the latter. (If you have good trash karma, the trash people may tell you the cops have asked about you.)

A real estate agent in California was busted and convicted of conspiracy to grow because of an empty shipping box that had previously held grow lights. The box was addressed to another person (according to the label), but lights of the same kind were found in the starter room at the project house, and the realtor had sold the land three times to growers, all of whom had been busted. The last time, the cops were angered by the agent and decided to look carefully at what was at his house and office.

A major conviction and property seizure were obtained when a cop said that the now-empty room in the barn had been a grow room, and that starter plants there had later been taken out into the country and planted in five separate gardens. The defendant had never been seen in any of the gardens, just "in the area" on his motorcycle, on public roads. In the room in question (according to the cops) was a pattern on the floor indicating big pots that had leaked excess fertilizer. That and one marijuana leaf in a spiderweb in a corner. Guilty.

D. BEAT THE HEAT GUIDELINES

1. There is no foolproof test to tell whether you're dealing with law enforcement personnel. It does no good to ask, "Are you a cop?" Cops are allowed to lie about being a cop. Narcs are allowed to do drugs. People you have known and trusted for years may have become informers. Entrapment is extremely hard to prove in court: you have to show that you had absolutely no interest in using/selling drugs, before the police invited you.

❋

2. When dealing with the police, keep your hands in view and don't make sudden moves.

❋

3. If detained or arrested, don't talk to the cops. Just give your name and address; say you're not going to answer any other questions; then ask for a lawyer.

❋

4. Police are only required to read you your rights if both: (a) you're detained and (b) they want to ask questions. If the cops ask you questions, but haven't detained you, and you answer their questions, your statements will be used against you. More importantly, if you are detained and the cops don't ask questions, but you talk to them, your statements will be used against you. Just because the police did not read you your rights, doesn't mean that you can beat your case.

❋

5. If you've been arrested and accidentally started answering questions, don't panic and give up. As soon as you remember your rights, state, "I want to remain silent now. I'm not going to say anything else without a lawyer."

❋

6. If the cops come to the door with an arrest warrant, step outside and lock the door. Cops can search any room you go into. Don't go back into the house to get your wallet or use the bathroom. If they do have an arrest warrant, hiding in your house isn't likely to help, so you might as well go, without letting them inside to search.

❋

7. Do not let the police into your home if they don't have a search warrant. Don't let them "invite themselves in." Make sure to say, "You do not have my consent to enter this house." If the cops say they do have a search warrant, take it and read it to see whether it's real. Look to see that it's signed, and has your correct address and a recent date. If the warrant is no good, tell them to go get another. The cops may threaten to tear the house apart if you make them get

another warrant, but they'll probably do that anyway, even if you let them in immediately.

8. If you're a minor, and one of your relatives or teachers is telling you to make statements to the police without your lawyer there, don't give in. Be respectful but firm. Don't let an authority figure talk you into giving up your rights.

9. Watch out for the Good Cop-Bad Cop routine. Remember that the "good cop" is likely to be someone of your own race or gender. Watch out for other common interrogation techniques, such as insisting that your buddies have snitched you off, so you might as well snitch on them; or claiming that the police have all the evi-

dence they need to convict you, and your best bet is to confess right away. It's easy for cops to play games with you when you're scared and alone.

10. If you're arrested with friends, make an agreement that no one will make statements to the police until everyone's been able to talk to a lawyer and decide what to do. Be aware of the paranoia which tends to set in after you've been separated.

11. In jail, don't talk to your cell mates about what happened to you, who was with you, or even whom you know. Stick to safe topics, such as: movies, music, sports, sex, etc.

E. POLICE INVESTIGATION

1. Techniques

The police rarely initiate an investigation on their own. Usually they're given a tip, information from a snitch, or other leads. Once they start, they have many options.

Legally, they can do quite a few things to check on activity or indoor cultivation. They can check with the electric company about unusually high use of electricity, search around the perimeter for grow light leaks, odors, or high traffic. They may also observe growing equipment or activities inside the house. Other investigative techniques include questioning neighbors and checking the auto licenses of visitors.

Police can also use thermal imaging, which measures the infrared energy coming from the house. The more heat an object emits, the better it shows up on a thermal image. Electric companies use the technique to show homeowners where they have heat leaks in their homes. Anything emitting heat shows up: warm-blooded animals, heaters, hot water pipes, and electric lights. High-wattage lamps show up brighter and in greater detail than low-energy-emitting objects. The units record the heat emitted at the object's surface: more heat will be emitted from the window of a hot room than a cool one.

Thermal imaging can be a potent weapon, but it has its limitations. It works best in one- or two-story buildings. An inner room of a third-story apartment, or the inner portion of a basement, is fairly immune to this kind of search. There may be an issue of illegal search if the cops use FLIR infrared camera systems.

The police are not allowed to trespass on the property immediately surrounding the home, nor can they use a ladder to peer over a fence. However, they can ask a neighbor to let them look while on his or her property. Though the police are constrained by the Fourth Amendment, private parties are not. For instance, a private party could use a ladder and binoculars to peer into a house or yard, an action police cannot legally take, and then report his or her findings to the police, who could apply for a search warrant based on the report.

To initiate an investigation, police sometimes get a warrant based on an "anonymous" tip or the information of a snitch. Of course, this immediately promotes corruption among the police, who often make the anonymous calls themselves or tell a person in trouble who to snitch off. "We know that you know N. He sold you this dope, right?" Recorder on. "I bought the dope from N."

a. Advanced Computer Sensing

I handled a case that began with a flyover at about 50,000 feet with the U-2 spy plane. The plane was equipped with colored differentiated x-ray spectroscopy, computer linked to LORAN. Every time the computer thought it saw the particular wavelength of light that is characteristic of marijuana and of no other plant, it noted the location. Later, the local narcs were given calls telling them where to look. The narcs went over the designated areas in fixed-wing aircraft and saw the pot.

When the case came to court, the local narc conveniently omitted any mention of the information he'd previously received. Only after he was thoroughly cross-examined by a team of highly skilled lawyers did that information come to light.

After a brief recess to summon the appropriate officials from the local naval weapons station, questioning resumed. The witness indicated that, in face, the equipment on board was protected by the National Security Act and that the court could go fly a kite or jump in the lake or some similar euphemism if it thought he (the witness) was going to tell it much of anything.

What he did tell the court was extremely upsetting. He said that the U-2 could look into your backyard from 50,000 feet and tell what you were eating for lunch, as well as probably the dates on the coins laying on the picnic table next to you (and possibly even the mint where each coin originated). It "certainly could identify marijuana as a specific plant in a specific location from those altitudes. The moral of the story: The helicopter you hear may be the electric company flying high-tension wires, but the spy eye in the sky may be spotting gardens.

ASK ED #7
THERMAL IMAGING June 97

I know that infrared detectors cannot look into a building. If I am growing in a room in middle of the house will excess heat be detected coming from the house?

Home Gardener

San Clemente, CA

The imager cannot "see" inside the house. It detects the heat at the surface—the walls and roof. The heat from a 1,000-watt lamp will be dispersed over the house and will not be detectable.

b. Cops: Smart or Stupid?

Occasionally outlaws learn through a simple twist of fate that some-body is watching them, knows what's going on, is hip to the situation. Perhaps the police have been told by an informant, seen the garden dur-ing a flyover, or discovered other legal or illegal means that something nasty is going on.

Based on my experience over the years and interviews with many growers, successful and unsuccessful, I think the facts must be analyzed from two points of view:

1. The police are extremely intelligent, devious, conniving, sophisticated, well equipped, and capable.

2. The police really are that dumb. They really do make clas-sic blunders. They really are stupid enough to send some-body up to the front door when they'd be better off sneak-ing around the back.

If you analyze the known facts from both of these bases, you may see that one or the other (or, damn it, sometimes both) explains the con-duct of the police.

Outdoor growers have told me that they've heard the whirr of hel-icopter blades at some point during the project and asked themselves the question, "Should I stay or should I go?" There is never a clear answer, but I've heard two proverbs on the subject that I appreciate:

Discretion is the better part of valor.

To live outside the law you must be careful. (Attributed to Lee Doyle, 1970.)

2. Blessed Anonymity

In the musical *Fiddler on the Roof,* one character asks, "Is there a bless-ing for the Czar?" The rabbi answers, "May God bless and keep the Czar—far away from us." This is also the best relationship an outlaw can have with the government. Act inconspicuously, look inconspicu-ous, and be inconspicuous. Your vehicle should be in good working order and be intelligently camouflaged. It should be neither too new, too old, nor too expensive. Your home should be kept neat. The garden and lawn should be typical of the neighborhood. Free growers do not brag, show conspicuous wealth, or make their friends envious.

Neighbors can be an outlaw's best friends or worst enemies, since they often are aware of what is going on before the suspect realizes he or she is in trouble. Smart growers have friendly relations with their neighbors and do not promote suspicion or hostility.

One case exemplifies stupid police tricks. The officers came to a house with a warrant authorizing them to search for drugs. Immediately upon entry, they went to a couch in the front room and put one gram of cocaine under a cushion. Apparently because they thought they were going to find many more drugs of other kinds in the house, no one bothered to write this piece of evidence down as Number 1 on their search warrant inventory.

After a futile search of the entire house, which turned up no other drugs of any kind (but lots of other bad stuff), the police went back to the couch and "discovered" this one gram of cocaine. It turned out that when they'd entered the basement, they'd taken a piece of plywood that was leaning up against the wall and put it down on the floor so they could scrutinize the wall surfaces. They didn't realize that they'd covered the floor safe with the plywood. They walked over the plywood and the safe for about 6 hours while they proceeded to dismantle the house,

even removing the wallboard from the upstairs bedroom walls. They never did find the safe.

🌿

In another case, the police narcotics agents went out to bust someone named by an informer. On arriving at the scene of the "covered buy," the officer in charge realized that he had busted this particular suspect about a year earlier. Rather than call things off and arrange other personnel for the deal, the officer decided to go ahead with it (apparently deciding to see just how stupid the suspect was).

The defendant confided later that he had thought the officer looked very familiar, but had placed him as a prior satisfied customer, rather than the officer who had arrested him on a previous occasion. Perhaps marijuana does affect your memory. You'd think no officer would be so bold, or so stupid, as to try to pull a scam on the same person twice. You'd also think the victim would recognize the cop who had busted him the preceding year.

🌿

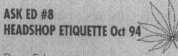

ASK ED #8
HEADSHOP ETIQUETTE Oct 94

Dear Ed,

Why is it when I walk into a "smoke" shop I cannot ask for the popular phrase "bong"? I must say "waterpipe." Is this lawfully acceptable?

Bill,

Tucson, AZ

_____

The law states that "drug paraphernalia" is illegal. The question then is, "What is drug paraphernalia? The answer, paraphernalia used for drugs. If its use is not *intended* for drugs then it is not drug paraphernalia. The only way to identify it as being intended for drug use is by naming it as such. Without a marijuana leaf or a title such as "bong" it could be used for anything.

Smoke shops do not carry any drug related literature and will not sell to you if you indicate that the goods are to be used for illegal purposes. They can lose the store, their property and their liberty if they do.

3. Sensitivity and Respect

Busted growers often tell me they knew the bust was coming. They saw the plane; chased away the "hiker;" fired a gun near hunters to scare them. Plainclothes cops sometimes go for a look around and leave footprints, cigarette butts, and other evidence (in one case, an empty doughnut box). If there's a particularly good place (bad for you) from which to observe the garden without being seen, the smart grower checks that place religiously to make sure he or she is not being watched.

Cops like to play cat-and-mouse. If they spot a garden in May, they may wait until October to visit. In a bust, starter plants can be just as big a headache as the monster females. In federal cases, sentencing revolves around plant *count*. Plant size, weight, sex, and yield are not considered.

If weight is a consideration in state law, the local cops will probably wait a while to try to catch the grower with some high-weight bud.

Smart dealers and growers keep their eyes and ears open. They stay aware of the normal and usual routine at the site (indoors or outdoors, rules are the same!) in case they spot something unusual. Even the most sensitive person may not have an easy time deciding if what she or he has seen/heard/felt was real or imagined, important or merely coincidental. There are very few sure signs you can use to tell if you're being watched. Even when one is faced with almost positive proof, one's inclination is to keep things going.

Many people sit in their attorneys' offices crying the blues about being busted after ignoring clear signs. It is safest to react swiftly and completely to any and all indications that the project has been compromised. If too many people—or *any* of the wrong people—know about the project, there's a very good chance that the grower will get a visit from cops, rip-off artists, or both.

In one case, a man was arrested with only 17 mediocre plants, but his records indicated that he had grown and sold $125,000 worth of marijuana 2 years earlier. Because he was keeping these records as a favor to a quadriplegic grower, who wasn't named in the records of sales (Who is "Doc"?) he was found guilty.

In another case, the police sifted through 20 boxes full of records and 600 computer disks and came up with a profile that allowed them to charge three persons (otherwise unknown to them) with conspiracy to cultivate, transport, and sell huge quantities of marijuana over a 6-year period. One of these defendants had to bite the bullet and plead guilty, exposing himself to a state prison term, even though no one had ever seen him smoke a joint and no one had seen him selling, had said he sold, or had caught him with any product whatsoever.

The records that his accomplices kept, coupled with sufficient corroboration of those records by his own accidentally discovered bank records, was sufficient to show the court that he was in fact a coparticipant and coconspirator.

Cops may talk to people who know about a suspect. Will a garden supply store snitch off the customer if asked by government agents? Can the store give your correct address? Credit card information is just like a searchlight pointing to you and your activities. Smart growers are discreet. They buy used items at flea markets, though the classifieds, or at sympathetic businesses.

The clerks behind the counters at grow supply stores and nurseries may give out customer names to the cops without a whisper or a word to you. If the customer uses a phony name and the cops note and trace the license plate of the vehicle in which the customer came to the store (true story!), it could end up in an affidavit in support of a search warrant. Delivery is a problem too. UPS cooperates with the cops and assists in busts by having a look around, giving information, and even setting up bogus deliveries complete with cops attached.

4. Record Keeping

People find themselves in deep trouble when police find the paperwork that they've left lying around. It's a police windfall to find records of what was going on, including names of individual plants, yields, characteristics, and, in the more tidy operations, perhaps even the price the product was sold for. Many dealers keep pay/owe data, financial records, and customer/supplier address/telephone books. Few kinds of evidence are more damning and harder to overcome than this type of record keeping.

I've been told that commercial pot growing requires business records. This argument implies that home growers have no reason for keeping garden notebooks around. However, they often do. Many marijuana growers have a close emotional attachment to their plants. In addition, much as with wine growing, in which the grapes and their treatment produce different flavors, each variety and, more subtly, each marijuana plant has a different taste and high. For the most part, this is controlled by genetic factors. Any kind of breeding program entails record keeping for particular plants.

The most devastating records the police can find are those that detail the sales of crops over the years. A dealer may find it necessary to keep some records to determine profit and loss, but I've never understood why they keep old records. Taxes are probably not being paid on sales, so there's no reason to keep them.

F. DEA OPERATIONS

In November 1989, the DEA served subpoenas on a number of high-tech garden stores. They demanded lists of customers from the stores. In order to give the owners an incentive to cooperate, they seized property and indicted the owners. Most of the establishments that found themselves in legal difficulties were caught in stings, during which the owners or the help admitted that the equipment could be used for marijuana cultivation or discussed the subject at greater length. Once armed with the customer lists and UPS logs, the DEA asked UPS to provide lists of deliveries to specific addresses. Most of the time, agents arrived at these residences without warrants and tried to talk their way in. In some cases they were able to obtain warrants, but most of these appear to have been thrown out by the courts.

In 1991, the DEA set up its own store (since closed) and encouraged its customers to talk about illegal activities. The DEA is still watching the stores. In 1992–93, they tried "administrative subpoenas," which had no legal authority. Still, many stores provided new customer lists. Because of continuing government actions, it's risky to purchase from some stores, and it's hard to know exactly which ones.

To check the bona fides of an establishment, a customer might ask whether the proprietors have ever been hassled and whether they had cooperated with government inquiries. If they say they have, or are unwilling to talk about it, the store may not be a good place for you to shop. If the salesperson implies or talks about illegal activities it is quite possible a sting operation is in progress or is being attempted.

Smart growers have learned never to purchase goods by mail order from stores, since stores ship via UPS, which keeps logs of all deliveries. If supplies are ordered by mail-order or internet, the goods should be sent to a safehouse. They should never be sent to the address where the garden is located. Purchases with credit cards or checks are avoided,

ASK ED #9
BOOKS THROUGH THE MAIL June 97

A friend ordered books to his house from one of the book companies in High Times. Now he's paranoid about growing because of the mail thing. I won't even get HT sent to my house. Am I paranoid? What do you think?

Concerned Grower

———

Booksellers have been advertising in *High Times* for years. If there were any suspicion that there was any kind of sting or police investigation because of book purchases, *High Times* would eliminate the ads and notify readers. I know most of the booksellers personally and think that they are people with integrity. I even own one of the companies, Quick Trading, which advertises in *Cannabis Culture*. I don't think that there is reason to fear persecution because of book purchases.

MAIL ORDER SEEDS

I've seen advertisements for northern lights and skunk #1 seeds in magazines and on the internet. Is there any danger in ordering these seeds?

Midnight Toker,

Internet

———

Buyer Beware. There are both legitimate and unscrupulous seed sellers advertising. Usually when a company has been around for a while you can surmise that it is legitimate, but that's not a guarantee.

There are several dangers in buying mail order seeds. They include being ripped off, fraudulent seeds and government stings. I know of no legitimate domestic companies, they are either frauds or stings. The seed companies in Holland, Germany and Canada may be legitimate, but they all have to get the seeds across the border. Most of them mail the seeds inconspicuously in first class mail envelopes. First class mail crosses porous borders but there is always the off chance that your package wasn't mailed (who knows? They say they mailed it), doesn't get through, or worse.

since these leave paper trails. When the problematic credit card is necessary, perhaps a friend would be willing to use his or her card to divert the paper trail. Using a friend's card also has its own downside, though: it introduces another trail that leads back to the grower, a person who knows the secret.

Growers don't use their vehicles to transport goods, since their license plates may be recorded at the places they visit. When they go to a garden store, they try to look like typical residents of the area. They purchase all the goods they can from nonsuspect garden shops, or even better, get used goods at flea markets or through classified ads in the newspapers.

G. RIP-OFFS

Suppose you're a grower and this situation occurs: You find thieves in your pot patch, or they find you. Are you prepared to shoot them (or be shot by them)?

Rip-off artists and cops believe the crop is worth a lot of money. Amateur and professional thieves are not uncommon. Almost any grower is a potential target for people who would burgle, rob, and even occasionally kill.

If you're caught with a weapon during the commission of a crime, you're in big trouble. A gun in the house while the pot is in the field might be enough to convict and increase your sentence. A defendant can usually count on the cops' using the guns as evidence of his/her vicious nature and

professional status. Sentences are increased by 1 to 10 years —in some cases, even more— just because the defendants possessed guns.

Pulling out and pointing a gun can be charged as a crime ranging from a misdemeanor—brandishing a weapon in a rude, angry, or threatening manner—to felony assault with a deadly weapon. Let's say you pull the gun and then walk the thief out of the area and she/he falls and gets hurt. The charges can escalate to kidnapping with bodily harm: life without possibility of parole. And of course, if you just run them off, will they return? With more people and/or more firepower?

🌿

CHAPTER 2:

What To Do if the Cops Come

A. Scenario 1:
   Cops Without a Warrant   **42**
   1. General Information   42
   2. Consent Searches   43
   3. Babysitting the House   43
   4. Exigent Circumstances   44

B. Scenario 2: Cops With a Warrant   **47**

C. The Scope of the Search   **47**

D. Bail   **48**

E. Clean-up   **50**

F. Photos   **51**

G. Return of Seized Items   **52**

H. Right to Remain Silent   **53**

I. Arraignment and
   Preliminary Hearing   **54**
   1. First Arraignment   54
   2. Preliminary Hearing   54

J. Forfeiture   **56**

K. Good Housekeeping   **57**

A. SCENARIO 1: COPS WITHOUT A WARRANT

1. General Information

Suppose two cops walk up to a door and say to the person who opens it, "We have reason to believe that you're growing marijuana. We would like to search the place. You can let us in now and we won't take you to jail. Or, if you don't cooperate, when we come back with the warrant, we'll kick the door in." What is that person to do?

Tell them to go get a warrant.

Here are the reasons: The judge may not grant them a search warrant based on the evidence they present. Even if the police are given one, the courts in later proceedings may find that the warrant wasn't good, because misrepresentations were made in obtaining it or for other reasons. However, if the person waives his or her rights and allows the police to conduct a search without a warrant, there's no chance to fight the search because there is no warrant to be contested.

It will take the police some time to get a warrant. Meanwhile, if things are present that could give the police the wrong impression, these can and should be destroyed. Lists of names that might appear to be pay/owe sheets; stray drugs; packaging material. Even if the warrant is not granted, the visit is still a signal to discontinue suspicious behavior. However, great care must be taken during the shutdown. The police may be curious about moving or similar activities and try to intimidate the suspect who is engaging in them.

If the police knock without a warrant, there is no law stating that you have to open the door or let them in. No matter how they may try to coerce you to open the door, unless they have a warrant it should not be opened. As soon as it is open, one cop is likely to say, "I smell marijuana." This simple statement, some courts may find, gives the police the right to search the premises. Opening the door is a no-win decision.

There is no issue and no hope of having the evidence suppressed if you agree or consent to a search. **The police may threaten, promise,** and lie, but if you don't consent, you have a chance that the law will later protect you from their excesses.

To insist that the cops must have a warrant is not evidence of your guilt. Your assertion of your rights can never be used as part of their justification for searching you. If you refuse to make their job easier, they may get tough with you, search anyway, and then lie about what was said or done. If you give in and sign a consent form, you have almost no chance of contesting the search. I've never understood why people make it easy for guys who are hassling them. These cops are not your friends, and will use everything they can to screw you later.

2. Consent Searches

If the police have sufficient probable cause to search and/or arrest you, they will do so with or without your consent. If you do consent to a search and they find contraband of any kind (or evidence of any crime), then you know for sure that you'll be arrested, and probably convicted, just because you gave up your constitutional protections against a police search without sufficient cause.

A law enforcement officer can search your home without a warrant if you, or someone who is apparently in control of your specific property, agrees to it. If you're staying in a hotel room or an apartment, the manager or landlord cannot give permission to search your room, but a maid who sees and tells violates no law. Parents can agree to the search of their children's rooms. They are not supposed to allow the search of the children's personal possessions, although the police and the parents generally ignore this nicety of law.

3. Babysitting the House

You don't have to allow the police to wait at or in your house while one of them goes to get a warrant. Don't give them any opportunity to claim that you consented to their presence at or in your house. If they have legally sufficient grounds for armed occupation, they'll do it. If they can't or don't get a warrant, you win. If you agree to save them the hassle, you lose whether or not they can get the warrant.

4. Exigent Circumstances

Anyone who is being detained or taken from one place to another in police custody, but not necessarily arrested, can be searched for weapons. This is a limited search of the exterior of your clothing. Only if the officer feels some hard object that he believes is or could be a weapon can they make you produce the item. If you are arrested, the police can do a full search at the scene of the arrest, or later when you're booked into jail.

ASK ED #10
VENTS AND ODORS Mar 94

Dear Ed,

We have a 6 ft. x 6 ft. basement garden. My main problem is that when my plants begin to flower, they also produce a very strong and sweet smell which fills my house. I like the smell but obviously cannot have it for safety reasons. I rigged a small fan to blow the smell out a small basement window. This solved the problem in the house, but the skunky smell was noticed by both cool and uncool friends alike when they were out in my yard.

Is there an inexpensive way to cure my problem?

Broke and Smelly,

Eldon, MO

Air ionizers load oxygen atoms with an extra electron, which is ready to jump from the atom to neutralize an odor molecule lacking the electron. When that happens the odor molecule ceases to smell and precipitates. This is the greasy dirt that can be seen surrounding ionizers. These devices work very well at eliminating odors near small gardens. The air cleaner should be placed at the entrance to the garden vent and perhaps a second one inside the vent pipe. The extra electrons in the charged air will jump onto odor particles floating in the air and will precipitate them onto the vent pipe. The air will be relieved of odor before it reaches the street.

A few years ago, an acquaintance of mine was implicated in an importing operation, but there was no clear evidence linking him to it. The police came; he refused to talk with them or let them in. Because they had no warrant and no probable cause, they never returned.

A client was visited by four plainclothes cops, who walked him into his house while neighbors watched. I called the cop shop and told the investigator that the episode had been seen by friendly neighbors. Although evidence was seized, no indictment followed.

A law enforcement officer can search your home without your consent and without a warrant in exigent situations (true emergencies). If the police are in hot pursuit of a fleeing felon, the search can't include the dresser drawers, but can include the closet, and anything in plain sight can be seized.

When an ionizer is placed in the grow area, the growing grass loses some of its odor and the buds have odor only when pinched. So, instead of placing the ionizers in the grow space, they set it up in the adjoining area so that any odor leaking from the grow space is eliminated. By placing the ionizer next to the vent most of the ionized air will be drawn into the vent cleaning the exiting air.

If the garden is bigger and ionizers don't do the job, an ozone generator may be the solution to your problem. They eliminate odors and purify the air. Instead of loading extra electrons on molecules and creating ions, these machines create ozone, an unstable form of oxygen. Gasses such as oxygen are ordinarily composed of two atoms which form the molecule, O_2. However, in the presence of electricity, they form O_3. This extra atom is ready to jump onto an odor molecule and oxidize it, neutralizing its smell. Ozone generators are capable of handling big odor problems.

Carbon filters are very effective in cleansing air as it is vented out. There are also odor purging gels and sprays which are very popular. Some of these are sold at indoor garden shops.

ASK ED #11
PARANOIA OR REALITY April 95

I have a small victory garden in my bathroom with a 400w HPS light.

One night I heard a lot of noise coming from outside so I opened my window and saw that the building next door was on fire. I called 911 and we all got out of the building and waited for the fire dept. to do their job. I saw one fireman go into my building with a couple of police officers. I was outside giving birth to a cow just knowing that they found my garden. They did not enter my apartment.

Does the Fourth Amendment protect me from this type of seizure or would I be SOL?

L.C.,
Brooklyn, N.Y.

Emergency crews can enter a premises under exigent circumstances and any evidence that they find which is in plain view can be used in a criminal court.

Two incidents come to mind. Several friends were smoking a hookah in the lower east side, a hip area of New York City, when police knocked on the door. They said there was a burglar in the courtyard and asked if they could enter through the apartment. The resident gave the police permission. The black officer seemed familiar with the odor and asked the white officer to stand outside the apartment as backup. The officer searched the courtyard futilely and then came to the living room containing smokers and smoke. He said, "Never let a cop in your apartment with the stuff just lying out." With that he grabbed into the bag, pulled out a small bud which he put in his shirt pocket, and left.

In the San Francisco Bay Area there was a fire on a property. The owners were not home and the firemen needed to enter a locked outbuilding. They called the police who opened it for them. Once inside the officers found that the roof had been replaced with clear plastic making a greenhouse filled with marijuana plants. The police took the plants but nothing else and never came back.

Each of these cases could have resulted in disaster. The police had a perfect right to be where they were under the doctrine of exigent circumstance or owner's permission. In an emergency the police are entitled to enter spaces for which they would usually require a warrant.

B. SCENARIO 2: COPS WITH A WARRANT

Suppose the police come in with a warrant, arrest a person, and demand cooperation—by which they mean a confession. First, they'll ask for a waiver of the suspect's Miranda rights, which are as follows: "You have the right to remain silent. Anything you say can be used against you in a court of law. You have the right to have an attorney present during questioning. If you cannot afford an attorney, you will be provided with one."

If the police do have a warrant, they may knock on the door or break in through it to scare you. In either case, the door should and will open. Even after the door is opened, you have some rights.

C. THE SCOPE OF THE SEARCH

If you're arrested in your home, an officer without a warrant can search only the area immediately around the place where you're arrested. She can search only for weapons that could be used offensively or evidence that could be destroyed. An officer can go from room to room to make sure no other people are in the house, but can search no further than that. This is why the officer can't open a desk drawer, but can open a closet door.

If an officer is legally searching for something, anything he sees in plain sight (without moving it or something else) that he recognizes as contraband, or evidence of a crime, can be seized.

When you're talking to cops, hide any heartfelt bad feelings toward them. Telling the cop who's searching your car that he has canine ancestors may only get you a harsh look, but it also may evolve into a lesson from the Rodney King School of Applied Manners. Always use your best manners when talking to any government official, even a clerk. They have the power of the government behind them. They can wield it to help you or to harm you. The most extreme public servants are cops who occasionally beat, arrest, and shoot people for no apparent reason other than their attitude. Be nice.

D. BAIL

Depending on the seriousness of the crime(s) you're charged with, and, in some cases, the degree of your threat to the public safety, you may be released on bail after being booked.

Bail is money or other securities (such as real property) deposited with the court to make sure that you will appear. Officers at the jail may be able to accept bail for the court. If you can't post (put up) the bail, you'll be kept in custody until a decision is made on your case.

If you're accused of a felony, you must deposit the full amount of bail. The money will be refunded if you make all the necessary court appearances. If you cannot afford to put up the bail, you may be able to get the transaction arranged through a bail bondsperson. They charge 10 percent of the bail amount as a nonrefundable fee. It's just like automobile insurance—you don't get the premium back even if you don't have an accident.

Instead of bail, you may be able to get released on your own recognizance (O.R.). This means you don't have to post bail because the judge believes you'll show up for all your court appearances. Some counties have O.R. projects to assist in the defendant's release without payment of bail, based on the defendant's ties to the community and previous record.

In setting the amount of bail, or deciding whether to release you on O.R., the judge will consider the nature of the crime you're charged with, your past record (if any), and your ties to the community, insofar as these are made known to the judge. Prepare and present affidavits, and bring live people to accompany your statement. Get your lawyer to check out your position and help you present the good points, however few they may be. This is an area where a little work will pay big dividends. Your ability to be assigned a reasonable bail (one you can afford to post) will allow you to be out and preparing to win the case. Make sure your lawyer has all the facts she needs at the proper time so you can show the judge that you can be trusted to return.

Anyone growing or possessing pot may get busted. People who are holding should have already thought about that and made plans for the cops' finding what is there, for bail, for the kids, dogs, cats, and fish.

The cops initially set the bail. A Friday arrest coupled with a cop who's really nasty could result in a very long weekend. It could be as late as Wednesday of the following week before you get a chance to convince a judge that $100,000 bail is not appropriate.

The issues at a bail hearing are simple: Will you come back to play the game, and will you be a danger to anyone in the community if released?

Federal courts have a system of pretrial supervision that allows most people to be out of custody on fairly reasonable terms pending trial. The exceptions are frightening. Although the constitutions of the United States and of most states seem by their terms to require and allow bail in noncapital offenses, laws that have been recently enacted allow the court to, in effect, sentence you to jail before you're convicted of any crime—by setting a bail that's impossible for you to post. Only changes made by Congress can stop this Alice-in-Wonderland judicial procedure: "Sentence first, trial later." You're entitled to a hearing on the issue of detention, but if the government goes after you in this way, it's very difficult to get a reasonable bail.

The cops' estimates of $5,000 per pound and 3 pounds of "biomass" per plant sometimes result in newspaper stories indicating millions of dollars in "street value" for your backyard crop. If unchallenged, these absurd estimates can give a judge the impression that you're a real criminal and therefore likely to split if released.

Until the paperwork goes to the local prosecutor for review and filing of the complaint, you are at the cops' mercy. A lot of local prosecutors simply go along with the cops' choice of crimes, and it may be a long time before you have an opportunity to show that the plants in the garden weren't really yours, and certainly aren't worth a million dollars, as the cops told the newspapers.

Bail is important. It takes money, obviously, and usually the title to some real property. Your lawyer can usually suggest a bondsperson. I can usually get my favorite one to immediately write a bond and spring my client, and get the money to her later. I therefore recommend her to my clients, along with a few other choices. If your lawyer doesn't know a local bondsperson, he either isn't a local practitioner or doesn't practice much criminal law.

> Anyone who was involved with the project should not go to post bail. One sorry character went to the jail to bail out his friends and was recognized by the cop from the photos the arresting officers had taken. He was arrested on the spot, and his efforts to bail out his two friends turned into arranging bail for three.
>
>

If you post bail and secure it with some assets, such as money or a car, the court and/or the prosecutor may ask rude questions as to where the assets came from. The source of the money or property must be "clean," or it could be forfeited. The property should start and end with a clean paper trail, and come from a person not implicated in any bad business. Parents or friends can loan money they obtained from a legitimate, documented source (such as the sale of something, or a bank or personal loan, or whatever).

When money is borrowed from someone to post bail, the paperwork must be done. Real loans are cemented with a written note, with the date of the loan, the due date (loans are paid back), a face amount, a rate of interest (if there is any), and signatures. If the courts ask, the money must be "clean," with a good paper trail, or the money too will be lost, with no gain of freedom.

E. CLEAN-UP

A good friend who is ready to help in case of legal necessity is a near-necessity. Such people don't need to know about the business in detail, but shouldn't be upset about it. They can help get money and signatures for bail; they can deal with the broken-into house and the terrorized pets.

This good friend should also have instructions to go to the house and make sure it's secure. He or she should close the door (or nail up a board if it's really bad), get the dog if the cops haven't shot it, feed the cats if they haven't been terrorized or shot or both (this is sometimes done "for officer safety"!), and then get a camera and take the "after" photographs A.S.A.P., given that this friend must also deal with the bail, the kids, and so on. The order is: all at once, immediately. It will be appreciated later.

This does not mean your friend goes and removes evidence or cleans your house up. Remember, it was the owner's duty to keep things looking marvelous. When the cops bust an outdoor project, they'll try to determine who is responsible, then try to go to that person's house to search for more evidence of cultivation and sales. They often find exactly what they say they expect to find: dope, scales, money, paperwork, guns, names and addresses of other people. Since the cops do "reasonably expect" to find contraband and/or evidence of the commission of a felony, the law will generally allow them to make a visit to the grower's home.

If there are records of bank accounts at the house, the cops are likely to find them and investigate. Cash deposits are noted and questioned. Crude attempts to launder the proceeds from a dope-growing or sales operation may form the basis for new and intricate felony charges.

F. PHOTOS

Don't clean up until after you take detailed photographs of the scene. Important details may not be apparent at the time, but the photos are a record you may be able to use to your benefit.

A field investigation video made by a defense expert showed that the defendant had put out a salt lick to attract deer—to a grow site? Get real!—which led to the successful defense contention that someone else had committed the crime.

When the "before" photo of an antique handgun was contrasted with an "after" photo showing its clear absence, the jury had serious doubts about the officers' credibility in other, more important matters.

Defendants regularly complain most bitterly about the theft that they believe the cops committed while serving the warrant. The law requires that the police leave a receipt for everything they take. The receipt should be detailed enough to identify each, every, any, and all of those items of "evidence" seized.

When the police raid a house and then things are missing, stolen items should be documented as carefully as possible and a formal complaint should be made. There is a good chance that the prosecutor or head cop will not believe the complaint and/or will not care. He or she may even be in on the deal, receiving some of the loot. Seized items often are not returned to the owners at the close of the case; instead, they are sold and the proceeds divided between the cops and the prosecutor or used for a party.

G. RETURN OF SEIZED ITEMS

The law allows the cops to seize evidence (things that prove something) or contraband (the drugs, scales, packaging, or containers). Unless a separate civil forfeiture is undertaken, the cops can keep nothing, not even those items purchased with drug proceeds (the TV, stereo, car, whatever) or used to facilitate the commission of the offense. These cannot be legally kept by the authorities after their value as evidence of your crime has been exhausted. This means that when the case is over, most of this stuff can be returned if the defendant requests it.

If the cops take your wallet, credit cards, identification, and so on, their return can be requested. Usually the prosecutor demands a stipulation (agreement) that other secondary evidence (such as a photo or a photocopy) can be used as "evidence." The prosecutor may agree, or the defense attorney can make a motion in court and try to get the judge to order the return of the items.

The other solution when the cops take your license and credit cards is to officially say they've been lost and get replacements. Most of the time this is easier, quicker, and cheaper than trying to wrestle with the cops and the prosecutor.

H. RIGHT TO REMAIN SILENT

You do not have to talk to the police, you have the right to an attorney, and everything you say may be held against you. The Bill of Rights was created for a reason: to protect people from the power of the state. When people waive their rights, they're giving up precious liberties. You should never agree to talk to the police. They will pervert everything you say, forget to mention or discount any information you give them that might exonerate you. Talking with them gives you no advantage. They're not permitted to make a deal, no matter what they say—"We can't promise anything but we'll put in a good word for you," or "This will make it easier." They may seem sympathetic while they make a bust, but on the stand in court they'll try to make things sound as bad as possible. Why should you talk to your enemy? These guys want to put you in jail. You should have nothing to do with them.

It's true that the police have some options and can give you a hard time if you resist their requests for cooperation. For instance, in California, for some offenses, they can choose between citing you and arresting you, so they might say, "If you cooperate, you won't have to go to jail now. We just give you a ticket for a court date. Otherwise, we might have to arrest your wife too, and place your kids in foster care." Most of this is bullshit, an attempt to coerce you into confessing and naming other people.

So the answer to the question, "Do you waive your rights?" should be a resounding "No." Tell the police, "I don't want to talk to you. I would like to call my attorney." If you don't have a lawyer, you should say, "I don't want to talk to you. I would like to talk to an attorney." You should try to do this in the presence of other people so that there can be no confusing of the issue when it gets to court. If the police try to coerce a confession, and it is shown that the confession was not willingly given, but was extorted, the case could get thrown out. No matter how abusive, scary, coercive, or bullying the police are, you should never waive your rights.

I. ARRAIGNMENT AND PRELIMINARY HEARING

1. First Arraignment

An arraignment is an appearance before a magistrate (judge) in a superior, municipal, or justice court, where the defendant is told officially of the charges against him. Arrestees have a right to be arraigned without unnecessary delay, usually within two court days after being arrested; otherwise, they should be released. A defendant can arrange a self-surrender by sending a letter to the court and the district attorney, offering to show up. This may save you the trouble of arrest and bail.

At the arraignment, an attorney will be appointed if the defendant cannot afford to hire one. The bail can also be raised or lowered. At this time, release on O.R. is considered, even if it was turned down before.

If the defendant is charged with a misdemeanor, he can plead guilty or not guilty to the charge at the arraignment. If the court approves, the plea can be "nolo contendere," which means "no contest" to the charges against you. Legally, it's the same as pleading guilty, except that it can't be used in civil litigation.

Before pleading guilty to some first-time misdemeanor offense (such as family violence, alcohol, or drug cases), defendants may want to find out if the state/county has a "diversion" (drug diversion) program. Under these programs, the court may order the defendant to get medical treatment and counseling, or perform community service, instead of being fined or sent to jail.

If misdemeanor charges are not dropped, a trial will be held in municipal court at a later time. If the charge is a felony, the next court appearance will be a preliminary hearing.

2. Preliminary Hearing

A preliminary hearing is usually held within 10 days after the arraignment. At that hearing, the D.A.'s office must present evidence showing "strong suspicion" that a felony was committed and that the defendant committed it. This is done in order to convince the judge that you should be brought to trial.

If the felony charges are not dropped at the preliminary hearing, there will be a second arraignment. This arraignment is held in superior court, where your trial will also be held at a later date and time.

It is at the preliminary hearing that the court decides whether there is enough evidence to hold a person for trial. The term for this is "probable cause." This means the police just have to prove that it was likely that the suspect committed the offense in order for her to be brought to trial. This proceeding is very important. It is here that the defense makes motions (asks the court to consider) to exclude illegal warrants and illegally gathered evidence. In some courts, if these motions are not made at this time, the defendant loses the right to appeal the court's decisions on these bases, even if the reasons are valid.

The preliminary hearing is the best time to beat a case. The whole legal proceeding is nipped in the bud, so long, drawn-out, expensive

---

One disabled Vietnam vet had calculated his life expectancy (shortened by various war-related factors) and his use patterns and was growing a lifetime supply. The cops found the paperwork and seized it without knowing what it was. When the suspect and his attorney reviewed the evidence, the defense was obvious (and successful), and 240 marijuana plants were found to be for personal use.

On the other side of the scales, so to speak, were the poor growers with historically significant scales (old, old, high-school-chemistry/yard-sale items) and hundreds of very small plastic lock-top Baggies, remnants of a coin-collecting hobby of yesteryear. The court needed to be rather forcefully shown that if one defendant really did have a 200-pound crop, she wouldn't sell it in 1-gram bags. If she had done so in the past, and was intending to do so with this pot, it would create a nonstop flow of customers night and day, deal lists, lots of cash, pre-bagged pot—all the bad stuff. The prosecutor hoped his fishing expedition would bring forth admissions of white-powder dealing (in some former life, I guess), but he was unsuccessful and the case was resolved very favorably.

legal proceedings are eliminated. If there is a good case for motions, the opportunity should not be missed and it should be handled by a high-quality lawyer.

J. FORFEITURE

To seize and forfeit property, the government must present the owner with a notice of the intended forfeiture. Once the government does so, the owner must file a document with the appropriate court within a very short time, usually 10 days. This is an absolute necessity for anyone who hopes to contest the seizure and avoid the forfeiture. People should be prepared in two ways: First, be prepared to file (or have someone else file) the claim within the brief time the statute allows. Second, be prepared for the bust so you aren't exposed to unwarranted seizures and forfeitures in the first place.

The owner may be faced with the dilemma of whether or not to claim the money or property seized. If you've made your preparations properly, you should be able to decide quickly and correctly whether there is any chance of recovery. This revolves around your ability to answer the questions of where, when, how, and from whom the property came to you without undue embarrassment. Preparedness is vital because when money or property is seized, the paperwork and excuses had better be already in place.

Many pot cultivation cases today are conceived, planned, and executed with forfeitures in the minds of the cops and/or the prosecutor. Most police agencies view forfeitures as a lucrative source of funds in this time of ever-tightening budgets.

Most cop shops have one specially trained person whose job is to take as much stuff as he or she legally can. These people are not fair and are not seeking justice, so things get ugly fast.

Most prosecutors also have an assistant or deputy prosecutor in charge of forfeitures. These people are often unskilled in civil litigation, since they are otherwise engaged in criminal cases. In my county, the job was given to the office geek because nobody wanted it. Fighting over people's money is what civil law is usually about for lawyers.

ASK ED #12
FORFEITURE Nov 94

Dear Ed,

If a person was caught with just one plant growing on his/her property could the authorities seize the real estate?

Hillside Cultivator,

Los Angeles, CA

Yes. Under federal law there is a "zero tolerance" policy. Boats and cars can be seized for "transportation" even of a single joint and real property (house and land) for manufacture (cultivation), or sales.

Criminal lawyers, however, usually view the debate over life and liberty as more critical than the money. That's why they're not in an insurance defense firm, or chasing ambulances. A civil lawyer may be required for the civil litigation.

The cops and prosecutors are ready, willing, and able to take toys, cars, and homes if the suspect is not prepared.

K. GOOD HOUSEKEEPING

Should the cops come to your little corner of the world, the scene they find will be, to some greater or lesser degree, fixed in time. Recorded in photographs, videotapes, evidence lists, diagrams, and police reports, that scene will be referenced by the cops, prosecutor, judge, and jury, as well as your attorney, throughout the case.

That's why it's vitally important that the scene the cops find truly reflects your innocence, lack of sophistication, desire to grow only for personal use, medical necessity for growing or use, or whatever the defense hopes the judge and jury would like to hear and would believe about you.

Large-scale growers and dealers, who have all the nasty stuff around that proves their status, are usually difficult to defend. Platform and triple-beam-balance scales, lots of Baggies, and the like require great explanations. Smart people don't keep a history of their cultivation or dealing. That includes photographs of prior deals and crops, diaries of the deepest, darkest secrets, including the deals, and the Eternal-Hope Seed Bank from 20 years of saving seeds.

CHAPTER 3:

The Search

A. General Information   60

B. Illegal Searches   60

C. Expectation of Privacy   61

D. Curtilage   62

E. Standing   63

A. GENERAL INFORMATION

A law enforcement officer can search you, your clothes, your purse and/or wallet, your car, and your home. The officer can make a search if you consent, with a search warrant, or under exigent (emergency) circumstances. The officer can, under some circumstances, search you without either your consent or a warrant.

If you're arrested, the cops can search you without further warrant or cause. This search is limited to weapons, evidence, or illegal or stolen goods. In general, this search must be of your person, or areas closely related in time and place to the offense you were arrested for.

If you're arrested and taken to jail, you may be subjected to a full search, including your most intimate body cavities, without any further supervision or paperwork. You have a right to be searched in a manner that is not offensive to common decency, usually meaning that female officers search female arrestees. Ladies, if any men want to search you or to be present when you're being intimately searched, scream like hell and demand to see the highest-ranking official who is available. Sexual molestation is not an appropriate part of an arrest for any crime. Custodial voyeurism is not legal.

You have much less protection from police intrusions into your life if you're driving your car. Any time the police stop your car for any legitimate reason, any contraband they see or smell could lead to a search and to your arrest without a warrant.

B. ILLEGAL SEARCHES

If you, your home, or your car is searched illegally, a judge may say that any evidence found during the search cannot be used against you in court. In order to punish the police for illegal conduct and to protect citizens' rights, the "fruits," or results, of an illegal search are not admitted into evidence in court. This is called suppressing the evidence; it's an increasingly rare occurrence.

If neither you nor your lawyer objects to the evidence before or at the trial, the court will allow that evidence to be used against you. The court will not say on its own that the police violated the law. You must object to the evidence and ask the court to throw it out. If you don't make a pretrial motion to suppress the evidence, you can't say on appeal that the search was illegal. You must pressure your lawyer to carefully consider all possible grounds for suppression of evidence. Don't let the lawyer say, "I don't think you'll win, so I won't try." If there's any reasonable theory, make the motion. You can't win if you don't play.

C. EXPECTATION OF PRIVACY

The courts have decided that the Constitution protects us from police searches only in certain circumstances. The Constitution guarantees the right of the people to be secure in their persons, homes, and effects from searches without a warrant that is sworn by the cops and signed by a magistrate.

The law recognizes your rights to keep the cops out in circumstances where you have a reasonable expectation of privacy. This must be subjectively held, which means you must believe the cops are invading a protected area. In addition, you must objectively manifest this belief of yours. This means you've got to make some effort to keep people (and the cops) from seeing that which you claim is private. If the grower has taken no precautions to conceal the crop, the law will have trouble finding a legitimate expectation of privacy. The last part of the "reasonable" equation is that society must be willing to recognize privacy as a legitimate concern. Many people believe that too many bad crooks get off if we stop the cops from doing something on the order of battering down the doors of crack houses, so we shouldn't stop them, and they need not have any reason to intrude.

Concrete examples of reasonable, protected interests are backyard fences and greenhouses. If the fence is there, it is evidence of your expectation of privacy. If the plants grow up over the fence, steps haven't been taken to objectively manifest the expectation of privacy, and the case is lost. It's a much closer case if the cops look over or through a fence.

Cops suspect all greenhouses of containing pot. It doesn't matter if you are a member of the Indoor Orchid Growers of America, raise and sell tomatoes year-round, or propagate world-class roses. If you have a greenhouse, the cops all think you grow pot somewhere, somehow. Though the law does not make such an assumption, the cops regularly use the "open-fields doctrine" to trespass and inspect greenhouses. The United States Supreme Court has said you must have something covering your crop for you to have a manifest expectation of privacy. We all know about airplanes, so how could you expect it to be private if you don't cover it? Hard choices, no easy answers.

D. CURTILAGE

The law regarding searches of your house and land is based on the concept of curtilage. The courts have decided that your house is protected from unwarranted searches but that the rest of the world, including your property, is not. The idea that property beyond the curtilage is unprotected by the need for a warrant was initially promulgated in order to stop Prohibition-era bootleggers and moonshiners. Revenue agents roamed the open fields at will and the court ruled against suppression of the evidence. No warrant was needed unless the curtilage was invaded, regardless of the fences or "No Trespassing" signs everywhere.

The judge who wrote that opinion probably didn't foresee how the cops would use it. Squads of goon cops going house-to-house to search the entire property, save and except the curtilage, paints an ugly picture of Nazi Brown Shirts on the rampage. This occurred in Humboldt County, California, 1993. The ever-vigilant attorney, Ron Sinoway, was able to stop this practice when he showed the court that the cops there had violated people's basic rights. The cases were thrown out of court, but the judge, who seemed righteously indignant, did nothing to the cops.

Curtilage is the area that is associated with the everyday activities of the household. It includes the front and back yards (fenced or not) to some greater or lesser extent. The barn is not generally in the curtilage, but a garage may be, depending on whether it's attached or not and how close it is to the house.

In the oldest English cases, the curtilage is described as the area within a bow-shot of the front door (and presumably the back door), the theory being that I could use my bow to protect myself without waiting for you to break down the door. No shooting is allowed these days, but the concept of curtilage is still with us.

Historically, curtilage was defined as the area intimately associated with the common household endeavors and the domestic economy. Your personal-use vegetable garden or henhouse may be part of your curtilage. The way in which the land is fenced and cross-fenced may be significant. Today the definition usually refers to the backyard or a well-fenced front yard.

You can establish that the cops invaded your curtilage by presenting facts to the court that connect the area searched to your private household endeavors. A chair and table in the garden may show that it was a place of calm refuge and contemplation; you spent your leisure time there, resting. The swimming pool is probably in the curtilage, but if it's a fertilizer mixer, then it's probably not.

Cops often draw their own conclusions about whether or not the places they've visited are within your curtilage. Don't let them win this point without a challenge. What you considered to be and used as your front or back "yard" is as important as the number of feet between the greenhouse and your front door. Cases are won by a field investigation bearing out the relationship of the garden to the curtilage.

E. STANDING

The term "standing" refers, among other things, to a person's right to ask the court to suppress the evidence. Recent incarnations of the Supreme Court have decided that if your own individual rights have been violated by the cops, you may be able to eliminate the evidence from the trial. However, if it was not your place, or not your stuff, then what's it to you? Saying "It ain't mine" doesn't guarantee that the jury will agree. However, it will surely remove your standing—that is, it will keep you from successfully challenging an illegal search.

You must show the court that your relationship to the place searched and/or the things seized was such that your personal toes have been trodden upon. If you say nothing beyond your name and address when questioned, the cop will establish standing for you: It's yours, you had it. That is normally enough. That the stuff was in your bag, car, or house is normally enough if you don't disclaim any interest in the particular box and its contents.

You don't need to admit knowledge of any crime or contraband in order to exercise your right to privacy and exclude others from a place or a package. If you have the right-now right of control, you have enough of a protected privacy interest to tell the cops "No" and make it stick.

It may be necessary to testify that you have standing in order to make a realistic motion to suppress. This testimony is not admissible at your trial unless you testify differently the second time. This is a major tactical decision, to be made with the help of a lawyer.

The most common standing problem occurs when the cops search A's house and find drugs and other stuff that indicates B is involved. Even if the cops had no warrant and have conducted an illegal search with no probable cause, B has no standing unless he can establish a personal expectation of privacy.

CHAPTER 4:

The Arrest

A. What Is an Arrest? **66**
   1. *What Is an Arrest Warrant?*   *66*
   2. *Should I Resist Arrest?*   *67*

B. Arrestees' Rights **67**

C. Questioning **68**

D. Detentions **68**

E. Post-Arrest **69**

F. Types of Charges **71**
   1. *Felonies*   *71*
   2. *Misdemeanors*   *71*
   3. *Infractions*   *71*

G. Clearing the Record **72**

H. Who Makes the Arrest? **73**

A. WHAT IS AN ARREST?

You are arrested if a law enforcement officer, or sometimes even a private citizen, takes you into custody. This means you're no longer a free person; you can't just walk away from the scene. The officer who arrests you should say that you're under arrest and tell you why. If you're stopped for a short time, you may have only been "detained," or held for questioning, rather than being arrested. Do not respond to questions such as "What do you think you did?" Ask questions if you want, but don't give information beyond what is necessary.

1. What Is an Arrest Warrant?

An arrest warrant is a piece of paper telling law enforcement officers to arrest a certain person. The arrest warrant must be signed by a judge or magistrate. The judge must have good reason to believe that the person named in the warrant committed a crime. If the suspect is unknown, a name like "John Doe" can be used, but the warrant must contain a particular description good enough to allow any cop to (probably) recognize you as the person described. If the cops have a John Doe warrant for the 6-foot-tall, 180-pound, dark-haired guy living at 123 Bust Street, they will look at you and ask your address. If you match the description, you go with them. If it's close, but ultimately not you, you may be released later, but the stash you were caught with probably sticks around. You can be detained while the cops check it out.

Once an arrest warrant has been issued, any law enforcement officer in the state can arrest the suspect. This can happen even if that officer doesn't have a copy of the warrant. The "statute of limitations" applies only to whether or not you are charged with a crime. There is no time limitation on using a warrant to make an arrest.

An arrest warrant must be issued before you can be taken into custody at your home. You can be arrested at home without a warrant only if the police have exigent (emergency) circumstances, such as escape prevention, citizen endangerment, or destruction of property or evidence, or if you are at home and committing a felony in the officers' presence.

2. Should I Resist Arrest?

A law enforcement officer can and will use whatever force is necessary to overcome your resistance, to arrest you, and to prevent your escape. A law enforcement officer can pin you to the ground during an arrest. Deadly force, such as shooting, can be used if the officer thinks you'll kill him or seriously hurt someone else. For your own safety, never resist arrest or detention.

Physically resisting arrest or detention is a serious crime. You can be charged with a misdemeanor or even a felony in addition to the crime for which you're being arrested. Even innocent people who are wrongly accused go to jail—contempt of cop. Acquitted on the substantive charge?

Too bad about the resisting-arrest charge.

A felony arrest warrant can be served at any time of the day or night. A misdemeanor arrest warrant usually cannot be served between 10:00 p.m. and 6:00 a.m., unless otherwise stated.

A traffic warrant can be served on you any time you can be found, usually in your car.

If the law enforcement officers have an arrest warrant, you have a right to see it. If they don't have one, you have a right to see it as soon as they can get it. They won't give a damn about showing it to you, and unless you can show that you were injured (prejudiced) somehow by their refusal, you lose.

B. ARRESTEES' RIGHTS

Police question you as part of their investigation, often without telling you your rights. Whether or not you have actually been arrested and/or taken into custody, you have the right to remain silent. You don't have to answer any questions. You must provide the police with your name and address; you must show identification. Before the cops interrogate you, you should be given your Miranda warnings. You should be told:

1. You have the right to remain silent.

2. Anything you say may be used against you (everything you say will be used against you).

3. You have the right to talk to a lawyer before being questioned, and to have a lawyer present while you are questioned.

4. If you cannot afford to hire a lawyer, one will be appointed for you.

If you are not given these warnings ("Mirandized"), your lawyer can and should ask that any and all statements made to the police not be used against you in a court of law. This does not mean that your case will be dismissed.

C. QUESTIONING

If you're not in custody (detained or arrested), the cops don't have to tell you your rights. Don't talk anyway. Don't play a game with the cops and hope your statement will later be suppressed.

Once the Miranda warnings have been given, you will be questioned only if you voluntarily give up your rights. The cops usually have you sign a waiver indicating that you understand what you're giving up.

You can stop the questioning at any time if you change your mind, as soon as you tell the police that you want it to end and/or that you want a lawyer.

D. DETENTIONS

You can be detained and questioned by the police for a brief investigation. The person detaining you must have reason to believe that you're involved in some criminal activity connected with a crime that has occurred, is occurring, or is about to occur. A police officer might be able to detain a person carrying a large box near the site of a recent burglary, or a hiker with a shovel and fertilizer near a garden. A customs inspector can detain you to search for illegal goods. Shopkeepers can detain you if they suspect you're ripping them off. Librarians can detain you if they suspect you've stolen a book. Like being arrested, being detained limits your freedom to walk away. However, a detention must be only for a short time. It usually occurs in a public place and does not involve going anywhere.

Once you've been detained, a law enforcement officer can do a patdown search. This means he can feel for weapons from outside your clothes. He may not go into your pockets without further probable cause. If you're arrested, the officer can search for anything else you have on you.

You have certain rights when you're detained, but the law does not require law enforcement officers to tell you about them. Although you should tell a law enforcement officer who you are and where you live, you can refuse to answer other questions. You can have a lawyer present while you're detained, but you're not entitled to free legal assistance. Make the cops an offer to come see them with your lawyer if they want to talk to you about some crime. Do not agree to go to some "more convenient" place. Ask if you can leave. If not, why not?

E. POST-ARREST

The police can require you to give certain physical evidence without letting you talk to an attorney first. If you're suspected of driving under the influence of alcohol, or of a drug, you may have to take a test to measure the amount of substance in your system. In California, if you refuse, you can lose your driver's license for up to one year. If you refuse a handwriting sample, or hair or fingerprints, the prosecutor will later say you did so because you knew you were guilty, and get a court order anyway.

After you're arrested, you can call a lawyer, a family member, a friend, a bail bondsperson, or any two people. You have the right to make and complete two free phone calls in your local dialing area within three hours of your arrest. This right belongs to everyone, citizen as well as noncitizen, upon arrest. Once they book you, you have a right to make the calls immediately—but ask, don't insist, or they will screw with you. The cops do keep track of who you call, and probably listen to your conversation.

ASK ED #13
CUTTINGS AND FEDERAL LAW July 94

Dear Ed,

I am aware of the federal guidelines concerning minimum mandatory sentencing which mandates a minimum sentence of five years if you are caught with 100 or more plants. If you were to get busted and have taken cuttings at what point would they be considered plants?

Stoned But Concerned,

Indian Wells, CA

Most federal district courts have considered cuttings as plants when they are "viable", that is, have roots, and do not need special care.

The federal guidelines state 49 or fewer plants are considered as 100 grams each for sentencing purposes no matter what their weight is, unless they weigh more. Then actual weight is used. Fifty or more plants are considered as 1000 grams, one kilogram each. One hundred kilograms or more is punishable by a minimum sentence of 5 years with 15 percent off for good behavior. One thousand plants or more (even tiny seedlings or rooted cuttings) draw a mandatory minimum of 10 years.

F. TYPES OF CHARGES

You can be arrested if you're suspected of committing a crime—a felony or a misdemeanor—or as an accessory for helping in the planning or commission of a crime or aiding someone to escape an arrest or conviction.

1. Felonies

A felony is usually defined as a crime punishable by imprisonment in state prison or by death. Murder, armed robbery, rape, and so on are felonies. So is cultivation of any number of marijuana plants or sale of any amount in all U.S. states, territories, and so on. Possession may be a misdemeanor or a felony depending on the quantity, the intent, and individual state laws. Both possession and cultivation are also federal crimes.

2. Misdemeanors

Crimes that aren't felonies are misdemeanors, unless they are infractions. Misdemeanors are punishable by a term of incarceration in the county jail or by a fine, or by both. Shoplifting and disturbing the peace are misdemeanors. In states with decriminalized marijuana possession laws, simple possession of small amounts is usually a misdemeanor or an infraction.

3. Infractions

Infractions are "petty offenses." They are minor. Usually a guilty verdict results in a fine instead of incarceration. Many vehicle code violations, such as jaywalking or illegal parking, are infractions. Instead of being arrested and taken into custody for committing infractions or certain misdemeanors, such as possession of less than an ounce of marijuana in California and some other states, suspects are asked to sign a citation or a notice to appear. When you sign a citation, you're not admitting guilt. You're only promising to show up in court at a specified date and time. If you have no ID or refuse to sign the citation, then you probably will end up being taken into custody.

G. CLEARING THE RECORD

After you're arrested, you'll be questioned. If the police are convinced that you haven't committed a crime before any charges are filed, you'll be given a written release. Your arrest will be considered a detention rather than recorded as an arrest. If the police are not convinced, you may be booked and released on bail, or possibly arraigned and given a hearing or a court date.

Once you're booked, your arrest is written into official police records. You'll be fingerprinted and photographed for the record. Records are checked for outstanding warrants against you, and your fingerprints are compared, by computer matching systems, with those already on file.

Information in your arrest record tells when and why you were arrested, whether the charges against you were dropped or whether you were convicted of the charges in a court of law, and what was the disposition of the case.

Pleading guilty and being found guilty after a trial both count as convictions, as does a "no contest" plea. If you're convicted of committing certain misdemeanors, serve your time, and complete probation and/or stay out of trouble for 1 year, you may be able to have the conviction removed from your record for such purposes as background checks for employment.

Local police departments and the state department of justice keep all arrest records. The law says that they can't show your arrest records to anyone except law enforcement agencies and certain employers that have a legal right to know. A personnel official at a hospital or a similar institution can see your record if you apply for a sensitive job, for instance a hospital job that involves dealing with patients, drugs, and so on.

You have a right to see your arrest record to make sure that all the statements in it are correct. The only way to remove an illegal or just plain wrong arrest from the record is to have the judge find that you're factually innocent. This involves showing the court that you did not commit the crime, not just proving reasonable doubt or dealing with technicalities. If you can convince a judge to do this, then you have ammunition with which to correct your arrest record and clear your name.

H. WHO MAKES THE ARREST?

Law enforcement officers make arrests. City and town police officers, county sheriffs, marshals, investigators from an attorney general's office or a district attorney's office, or Highway Patrol officers—and any other law enforcement officials—can and will arrest you, whether they are on or off duty, and whether or not they are in their home town or county. Cops from another state may only be acting as private citizens, but they too can arrest you and turn you over to the local cops.

These officers can arrest you even without an arrest warrant. All they need is "probable cause," which means good reason to believe you committed or tried to commit an offense in their presence. These officers don't even have to see you commit the offense.

Private security guards are not law enforcement officers, but they can arrest you as private citizens. A citizen who sees a misdemeanor or felony being attempted or committed can make a legal arrest as long as there is good reason to believe the person being arrested committed the crime. The citizen must take you to a police officer or a judge, who is required by law to take you into custody.

CHAPTER 5:

Choosing a Lawyer

A. Lawyers' Licenses   **76**

B. How to Choose a Lawyer   **76**
1. Finding Likely Prospects   76
2. Making Your Choice   78

C. Renter Beware   **80**

D. Qualities of Good Defense Lawyers   **82**

E. Do You Know Your Lawyer Yet?   **82**

F. Retainers   **84**

G. Fees   **84**

H. Do You Need a Public Defender?   **85**
1. P. D. Realities   85
2. Helping Your P. D.   86
3. My Appointed Attorney Won't Call Me Back!   87
4. Changing P. D.s   88

I. Lawyer–Client Relationships   **89**
1. Types of Relationships   89
2. What is Client Control?   90

A. LAWYERS' LICENSES

A case in a federal court can be defended by anyone admitted to practice law in any state and also in that district. The attorney has to swear that he will uphold the rules, follow the law, be respectful, and pay any fees in order to qualify to practice. Usually an out-of-the-area attorney must associate (hire) local counsel to assist to some greater or lesser degree, as needed or required by local court rules.

Cases prosecuted in state courts can be defended by any member of that state's bar or, again, by out-of-town talent associated with a local attorney, and admitted *pro hoc vice* (for that one case). You may not be able to get someone local who can do the job you need, but a local practitioner will save you money and will know his way around the court. He can be used in conjunction with an "imported" attorney.

B. HOW TO CHOOSE A LAWYER

1. Finding Likely Prospects

For good leads to a good attorney, try the membership rosters of some criminal defense–oriented groups. The National Association of Criminal Defense Lawyers is one such source. Each state has attorneys' associations. In California there are several groups, such as the California Public Defenders Association and the California Attorneys for Criminal Justice. NORML (National Organization for the Reform of Marijuana Laws) also has a referral service.

An important caveat is that anyone who can afford the dues can join any of these organizations. Some attorneys join everything in sight to network for clients, for status, and for referrals. The vast majority of lawyers in these groups, and in most others, are dedicated, knowledgeable specialists in professional criminal defense—your kind of people, with the access to specialized help and knowledge that you need.

Ask for recommendations from friends, coworkers, relatives, or employers. Business professionals, such as doctors, bankers, and teachers, as well as ministers, may be able to refer you to a lawyer. Look in the Yellow Pages of your telephone directory under "Attorneys" and "Attorney Referral Services." The person who takes your call will be able to refer you to someone who can assist you further or direct you to the proper area. A good reference from a satisfied former client is worth hours of time. However, be careful about hiring an attorney based on a glowing recommendation from someone who had a dissimilar case. Divorce, personal injury, and probate attorneys are probably not qualified to handle marijuana cultivation cases.

ASK ED #14
FAMM Aug 94

Dear Ed,

Could you provide me with the address of Families Against Mandatory Minimums? It is really a shame how the system works; deal with drugs you get life, if you are a violent criminal you get only months!

Nicole,

Decatur, GA

FAMM is one of the most effective lobbying groups on our side. It was founded a few years ago by Julie Stewart, whose brother is doing mandatory time, and has more than 23,000 members. FAMM coordinated testimony from lawyers and affected families at the U.S. Sentencing Commission hearings held last March.

FAMM's address:

Families Against Mandatory Minimums
1612 K St. NW #1400
Washington, D.C. 20006
Tel. 202-822-6700
Fax 202-822-6704
www.famm.org

Tell them Ed sent you.

Do you belong to a "legal insurance" plan individually, or through your employer, labor union, or credit union? If you have an employer, find out through the personnel department. Perhaps your plan provides for legal services by offering an attorney to represent you.

2. Making Your Choice

Choosing a lawyer is not a matter of diplomas on the wall, a well-appointed office waiting room, designer dresses, $2,000 suits, or a short haircut. Each case is different; each defendant is different; each lawyer is different. Finding a good match is difficult but possible. It's a lot like choosing a life companion from among many possibilities. They may be very much alike, but each will be different and attractive in his own way. And, like a spouse, this decision may be one you'll live with for the rest of your life.

Ask the attorney about her last jury trial for cultivation. Ask him to describe the last five or six marijuana cases he has taken to court. You don't need the names, just the cases, the issues, the strategy, the tactics, and the results. You should be able to spot and sift through bull this way. Don't be surprised if he is obviously uneasy; keep asking for specifics.

Ask the lawyer about himself. "War stories" from prior cases only celebrate victories. Attorneys rarely discuss losing cases with their clients. Every case—including yours—is different. If an attorney concentrates on his war stories and you can't get a straight answer about your case, he's probably not for you.

Don't pass up a lawyer just because she is new and inexperienced. Old and inexperienced may be worse. But do hire someone who regularly defends criminal cases, drug cases, pot cases, and/or pot-growing cases. If the lawyer is inexperienced, she may still be a good lawyer who will work hard, but perhaps you should adjust the fee. You shouldn't pay for the lawyer's education.

You can go to see most lawyers for a brief consultation. This should be free, but "brief" is the key word. Be prepared to talk or listen as required, and take all your paperwork with you.

Don't choose a less-than-enthusiastic lawyer. Personality does count. You must feel comfortable with this person, because you'll come to rely on him or her emotionally as well as legally. Pick someone who has some empathy toward you and your situation. A lawyer must have the spark of life, the "warm zeal" for defense, but must also remain a somewhat detached tactician.

When you're shopping for a lawyer, be aware of your own psychology. You'll want to be reassured by the person you interview, and will crave the slightest indication that you'll win the case and go free. Nevertheless, resist the impulse to hire the most optimistic player. No one can predict, let alone guarantee, the result of your case. Anyone who seems to do so is stretching the truth, probably to get you to cross the "green line"—the point where you start paying. If the attorney seems too enthusiastic, get his claims in writing (an informal opinion letter, perhaps). Later his opinion may change and you may get an expensive lesson in misplaced trust. If your attorney decides not to do something that you've discussed and that you believed was going to happen, be sure to get a real explanation—in writing if you suspect a sellout.

You'll probably decide which lawyer to hire before you or she has any police reports or court papers. A "realistic" assessment of your case, provided by an attorney without these documents, can only be a cruel fantasy. The most that a competent lawyer should do is suggest the possible strategies or tactical maneuvers that could be useful to your case.

Imagine yourself confiding your deepest, darkest secrets to this man or woman. Like a medical doctor, the lawyer often must know the truth, however bad. No lawyer should be judgmental or belittle you for your acts or omissions. You don't need another mother, or two judges on the case. You need someone who will work hard to learn and master the facts, research the law as necessary, figure out things to do that may get you off, and then do them well and effectively.

Shop around. You're entrusting this person with your life and your freedom. Talk openly about fees, strategies, experience, and anything else you think is relevant to making a good choice. You may be swayed to a choice because one lawyer drives a BMW and another drives a Jeep. The decision will probably be made because you feel comfortable with a particular person.

C. RENTER BEWARE

Attorneys are a lot like cars. You can get one out on the road for a few hundred dollars, but a reliable one, which also gives you a smooth ride, costs more—and there's no limit to what you can spend on an automobile. Lawyer-shoppers face the further problem that choosing a lawyer may be more like choosing a used car. Even an expensive lawyer can still be a lemon.

Be aware that your choice of an attorney will determine just how the case is pursued. A lawyer who doesn't know the law can do you irreparable damage by waiving rights, not making motions regarding police actions that might cause the case to be dismissed, or not representing you. When you're shopping around for the right attorney, there are some ways to sort through the lists.

It's best to choose an attorney who specializes in marijuana or drug cases, or at least in criminal cases. They can be asked about their record, their general strategies, whether they usually plead clients out or turn them into snitches. This may be the most important decision you'll ever make.

Before you hire a private attorney, you can make inquiries to the state board, the consumer affairs department, and the state bar to see if there are complaints or actions against him or her. The attorney's colleagues can be asked their opinions of him or her. If they have disparaging remarks to make, they'll usually couch them in subtleties, so you'll sometimes have to read between the lines. "Jones has a unique style, but hasn't yet perfected his technique" means he loses cases that could have been won. Former clients can also give you references. The attorney you're considering can also be asked to provide references.

Think of lawyers as if they were surgeons. You want to use one to cut away a disease. Certainly if you were planning on major surgery to fight a serious disease, you'd get the opinions of several doctors regarding the case. Don't be awed just because a person has professional credentials. Lawyers are humans, just like everyone else. They'll have different opinions about the case and will suggest different strategies.

C. RENTER BEWARE (continued)

The best attorneys are creative, knowledgeable, and enthusiastic. If an attorney lacks any of these qualities, he or she usually should not be considered. No one strategy is necessarily right or wrong; there may be several valid alternatives. It's up to you to decide which strategy suits you and which attorney seems most compatible with you. I'm always suspicious of attorneys who think they know it all and are not interested in input from the client. In my experience, clients often have interesting and useful insights that help make a case. The best attorneys I've worked with confer closely with their clients while putting the case together.

Local attorneys sometimes discourage clients from hiring out-of-town or well-known attorneys. Their theory is that a high-powered defense will in itself raise suspicions regarding the defendant. My experience watching judges and juries has not borne out that belief. I've found the courts to be impressed with good-quality counsel. They seem to feel that it reflects on the importance of the case, rather than on the defendant's guilt.

During the Vietnam War, the U.S. increased its troop strength incrementally, moving slowly from a few thousand soldiers to 300,000. This slow buildup gave the enemy time to adjust to the situation and learn how to deal with it. A marginal attorney might say, "Let me do the preliminary hearing and the motions; then if you don't win, get a trial lawyer." I think this is a bad strategy. Rather than increase force gradually, which gives the prosecutor time to prepare, you want to blast them out of the water as fast as possible. It will cost less in the long run, since less attorney time will be used, the case will end faster, and there will be less pressure on the defendant.

A good attorney may be able to quash the government case at the preliminary hearing and thus put an immediate end to the prosecution.

D. **QUALITIES OF GOOD DEFENSE LAWYERS**

Successful criminal defense requires the stamina of a fighter, the willingness to take on the state, the love of a good intellectual fight, and a passion for winning. Most good defense lawyers consider themselves outlaws; often they hang out with other outlaws.

Much like the knights of old England, your lawyer is a paid champion, sent to do battle with the forces of the government. The other side usually has the big horses, the best armor, and the white hats. If the knight you've personally chosen to champion your cause is too close to the political or social establishment, he may not have the requisite fighting spirit. I've never understood how someone who challenges and tries to defeat the prosecutor on an intensely personal basis can then ride home, lunch, or play golf with him or her. It seems to be a sellout to me.

How your lawyer looks may or may not matter. A good-looking lawyer isn't worth anything without all the other qualities we've discussed. Obviously, competence doesn't come with the purchase of clothes, cars, or office furniture. The best lawyers are often unaware of, or don't care about, those petty things. Your life and liberty may be worth the effort to look past appearances to the substance of the person.

Tony Serra, the role model for the movie "True Believer," has long hair, wears nondescript clothing, and drives old cars. Mike Stepanian, noted San Francisco attorney and author of "Pot Shots," has called pot defense lawyers the Samurai of the counterculture, and that captures somewhat the flavor of a good attorney.

E. **DO YOU KNOW YOUR LAWYER YET?**

It's not illegal, nor is it evidence of guilt, to know the law and its ramifications. Going to a reputable criminal defense attorney and paying for a consultation makes good sense. You must have a couple of dozen questions you'd like to ask someone who knows.

No lawyer can (or should) give you advice on how to break the law successfully, how to evade prosecution, or how to cover your ass if you're busted. Charges of obstructing justice, aiding and abetting, or counseling the commission of various felonies have all been brought against defense lawyers who were not careful as to what they said or to whom they said it. This is why good criminal defense attorneys are careful. If an attorney has a successful private practice, the chances are good that the cops have tried to bust him or her for some real or imagined indiscretion.

Lawyers must follow the rules of ethics. As a matter of basic self-protection, a lawyer will be very hesitant to advise you if no case is pending and you don't sound right, feel right, and look and smell right. You don't have to confess all your indiscretions to a lawyer. If your brother Joe is breaking the law, you might ask a lawyer about it. If you have a fictional scenario in mind that will help to illustrate your questions and make the answers meaningful, it's okay to talk about that. Often a person who is thinking about growing pot will consult a lawyer and decide that the risks and penalties outweigh the probable benefits and decide not to grow. (Remember the conspiracy laws!)

It's better to get the feel of a lawyer as a person when there's no emergency pending in your life. It's also better to get a realistic assessment of your contemplated actions than an after-the-fact monologue from the lawyer about how you screwed up.

Most attorneys don't charge for a brief consultation about a pending or potential case, because they want to be hired for that actual case. But if you haven't been busted and don't expect to be, you should pay the lawyer's regular hourly rate for a consultation.

Prepare all your questions and then, during the consultation, make notes and get new ideas. The difference between good and bad lawyers will be more evident if you're not stressed out and searching frantically for someone to save you. Ego-trippers, especially, are easier to spot when you're not twisted. The "Trust me, I can help you" aspect is not there, and the true grit becomes visible.

It's possible that you'll find one lawyer who's obviously better than the others you've seen. If you're fairly certain that this is the person you would turn to in case of a bust, then you can think about that great American institution, the lawyer on a retainer. If you give a lawyer money, she can treat it either as an opening move on a particular matter, or as a fee to insure her later availability.

The best lawyers tend to be the busiest, and may be busy elsewhere. A single lawyer or law firm can defend only a limited number of clients competently. Your retainer fee helps the lawyer pay the bills in lean times or pay for a toy or a trip, or buys you some number of hours of representation later, if you need them. The lawyer earns the money for being available if needed. If you do get busted, you know who to call. Lawyers are happy to hear from someone they know. Most important, they'll feel obligated to begin work immediately.

F. RETAINERS

Attorneys are required to tell the Feds if you pay more than $10,000.00 in cash. The fee for a decent attorney in a serious case will seriously exceed this limit. Simple problem, simple answer: Don't pay in cash. A check from you or from some third party is all the preparation it takes to avoid this potentially embarrassing problem.

G. FEES

Before hiring an attorney, you should discuss price, find out exactly what he will do for that price, and get a written statement and a receipt. People who wouldn't think twice about trying to negotiate the price of a stereo in a store often feel too cowed to discuss money with a lawyer. It somehow seems out of place to them. This works to the lawyer's advantage, and makes it easy for him to set a price. There is no reason for you not to discuss the price, the terms of payment, and in what form the fees are to be paid. In some cases, attorneys are required to report cash payments of as little as $3,000 to the government, so they should be paid by credit card or check.

Establish a budget with the lawyer. Revise it regularly; stay informed as to what your money has bought. There is a universal requirement that lawyers keep records of things they do and the time they spend on your case. Even in a flat-rate-fee arrangement, you should be able to see the file grow thicker, and the pleadings and paperwork from both sides should be given to you as a matter of course. You should keep abreast of your case. Even the busiest of lawyers can call you back, if necessary after business hours, or the paralegal assistant/secretary can meaningfully relay your concerns and answer your questions.

H. DO YOU NEED A PUBLIC DEFENDER?

The question of whether or not you can afford to hire a lawyer means simply this: Do you have money? Mom and Dad aren't required to help you. If you don't have a substantial bank account, a partially paid-for home, or a regular job, you probably qualify for the public defender. You don't have to mortgage your property or spend yourself into poverty for a lawyer. The public defender (or a court-appointed counsel from a list on a panel, or a private lawyer or law firm with a contract) will do his best for little or no money.

If you can't afford to hire your own lawyer, the court will appoint one for you. You may be required to pay some or all of the fees charged by this lawyer, usually less than $250. This depends on your financial status.

1. P.D. Realities

You do need the assistance of an attorney. The key word is "assistance." All the requirements we've discussed so far apply to a public defender as well.

Usually these lawyers are talented and dedicated. The problem is that they're underfunded and overworked. This means that a marijuana case may not get the attention it requires. This is understandable, especially if the overworked public defender or court-appointed lawyer is also handling murder 1, manslaughter, assault, and robbery cases, which are considered much more serious.

A defendant has several options, even if she has no money to spend on attorneys. You could shop around and try to make a deal to get the court to appoint the attorney of your choice. For instance, in one case of a married couple in California, the public defender was appointed to defend the wife. To avoid a conflict of interest, the husband could not use the P.D.'s office, so he shopped around for an attorney (who was paid by the state) until he found one who shared his idea of a defense.

Even if there's no choice but to use a P.D., all is not lost. A squeaky wheel gets the most attention. By letting the P.D. know that you're taking the case very seriously and that a certain level of service is expected, you may get much more attention.

At the very least, you have to tell the attorney the facts. In addition, you can be the "gofer" and research assistant. The only things that limit your participation are your interest and your lawyer's time and patience. Helping the attorney to prepare the case can save her enormous amounts of time, and gives you insight into how the battle is fought. Some things you can do are to develop a theory of the case, examine and critique the police and prosecution documents, make a detailed investigation of crime-scene data, find experts, and help locate and identify witnesses (but not serve subpoenas, since you're a party to the action).

All appointed attorneys are hideously overworked and disgustingly underpaid. Many counties prohibit public defenders from working overtime (the budget, you know) on the hundreds of cases they have. Some are great lawyers performing a valuable and noble public service; some are dweebs, punks, creeps, and dump trucks hiding from real work behind the skirts of a government paycheck.

The problems are these: (1) It's not always easy to tell what kind of lawyer has been assigned to you. (2) You'll have very little control over the particular attorney you get from the court. Even the great public defenders and Criminal Justice Act panel attorneys are far too busy to treat you like a private, paying client. Government funds for court-appointed attorneys have always been tight, and the prosecution's budget always outweighs that of the defense. With an appointed attorney, it's not a fair fight.

2. Helping Your P.D.

There are many ways you can help your (appointed or retained) attorney represent you well.

1. Be professional, helpful, and caring. Be on time for appointments with the lawyer. Get the names, addresses, and paperwork you have access to before they're needed. Communicate this information. Write it down so that you and your lawyer won't forget.

2. Be awake, involved, calm, and centered. It won't help to be overly emotional. Tears or yelling may be necessary to reach a real turd, but it's rare that they'll help.

3. Write things down. This may seem stupid, but your word that something was told, promised, planned, and so on will carry much more weight if your notepad shows when, and with whom, you discussed it. Such a trick also helps keep you calm in the crunch. When you get very upset, take a deep breath and make some notes.

3. My Appointed Attorney Won't Call Me Back!

If you've been pleasantly insistent, and have done everything you were supposed to do, you'll most likely be so unusual that your attorney will quit ducking your calls. If you call and are put off, call again. Make an appointment to call and talk. Attorneys have a legal duty to meet and confer with clients. It is partly up to you to make sure that your meeting is not just the one minute before your case is called in court each day. Be nice, but be insistent. Keep notes of when you called and who you spoke to.

If you feel you aren't being represented by your appointed lawyer, and he won't talk to you about the case, you may be able to have another one appointed. Here's what to do:

After too many unsuccessful attempts to see or talk to your attorney (or at least to some attorney from the office who is knowledgeable about your case), you can start to complain. How many times are too many? It depends on how complex the case is, and how soon you go to court again. An "interviewer" or an investigator may routinely be used to get your story, but you have a right (and an obligation to yourself) to talk to the lawyer. Only the lawyer can evaluate your case and give you legal advice. If you have diligently tried to see him, take notes on your attempts, then try to see a supervisor or even the office chief of staff.

This usually produces an upset attorney who's been ordered to see you. Better for her to be upset now than for you to be upset later on. If the lawyer is mad because she has to talk to you and explain your case, perhaps you should suggest she give the case to someone who will help you and not get mad about it.

4. Changing P.D.s

If all your efforts to communicate fail, and you come to court without having had any contact with the attorney, tell the judge. Have your notepad detailing the many, many attempts you made, and then you can make your attorney tell the court what the problems have been, why he hasn't talked to you, and when he will do so.

The judge will undoubtedly start by oozing praise for the attorney who's trying to sell you out. I've heard judges lie shamelessly to defendants about their feelings or opinions about a lawyer. The judge probably knows that the so-called attorney has not really represented anyone in years. However, a judge will say, "She's an experienced, competent attorney." What this may really mean is that the attorney has not yet been disbarred, but is neither competent nor experienced. The court is trying to protect the record. The judge is only interested in getting you in and out of his court A.S.A.P. and making whatever happens stick.

Reversals for incompetent counsel are very rare, even though incompetent attorneys abound. Don't let the judge talk you into withdrawing your objections to the lack of real assistance from your attorney. Be strong, ask for someone else, and make a record of your objections and efforts.

The grounds (the reasons you must allege) for getting a new attorney are that your wishes and desires about the defense of the case differ from those of your attorney and a conflict has arisen, so that you and he can't cooperate to prepare and present the defense you want to present. If your lawyer "thinks you'll be convicted," and therefore refuses to prepare a defense, get a new lawyer. You can tell the judge the problems in his chambers without the prosecutor present. This maintains confidentiality and protects your case. Please remember that the truth may be that you're screwed. Even so, your attorney should still try to get you off.

The obvious downside of asking for a new attorney is that you may get the very worst attorney, who is assigned to deal with difficult defendants. However, you may wind up with the best and brightest if you demonstrate that you're aware, awake, and interested. A fair amount of knowledge on your part may also persuade the powers that be that you're serious and that you deserve adequate representation.

Let me say without qualification that a bad public defender may be better by far than an expensive, incompetent private attorney. At least P.D.s practice criminal law exclusively, day after day, and have access to knowledgeable help. An alcoholic divorce lawyer may get a big fee and not only do nothing, but also know nothing.

I. LAWYER-CLIENT RELATIONSHIPS

1. Types of Relationships

There are no set rules that control how much or how little you participate in your defense. It's a matter of agreement and capabilities. Your attorney should be willing to discuss the degree of your participation.

Don't expect the attorney to give you a law school education, but a complete explanation of all the important issues is mandatory. If you have the desire, the next step is to read the relevant case law.

If you find, as many clients have, that your lawyer has changed from a gung-ho fighter to someone who tells you, "You're guilty, take the deal," be very careful. It's a common cheap trick for lawyers to take a case—and all your money—and, after doing little or no real work, to dump you to the Public Defender or try to plead you out. Lack of money is not a controlling factor. You have to be able to afford what you want done, but money is not a good enough reason in and of itself to dump you.

Even a competent, thorough defense attorney can't always win. If the facts are incriminating, there may be no defense against the charges. The true role of the defense attorney is to think up ways to get you off. Be careful that your attorney doesn't lie to you about your chances of winning just to get the case and then tell you later that you have no defense.

If you and the lawyer have talked about a motion to suppress, it should be made, heard, argued, and (if appropriate) denied by a judge. Your attorney should not say, "I thought it had no chance, so I didn't try."

As I've noted, the duty of the defense attorney is to think up ways to get you free. If you want to pursue any of these options, the attorney's job is to do the best preparation and presentation possible. If it turns out to have been an unsuccessful choice, at least it was your informed choice of action. It's often true that your strength and determination will motivate an attorney to do well, and just trying, just fighting hard, may turn up some angles that were not apparent at first blush. It's never too late to fight, according to some experienced, successful defendants.

Most good lawyers I know will take time to explain the justice system to you, to acquaint you with the basic principles, and to get some idea of your particular story. Don't expect to tell all during the first meeting. The relationship will grow and there will be time, soon, to talk some more.

2. *What Is Client Control?*

Client control occurs when a lawyer uses his superior knowledge and skills to steer the client in any particular direction that the lawyer wishes him or her to go. By steering the client's opinion for the sake of the attorney's own wishes, he is able to force or allow clients to plead guilty to crimes and sentences they do not deserve.

The problem for the layperson is that it's difficult to spot a lawyer who puts his interests before the client's. A second opinion is always acceptable to a real lawyer who's being square with you. Clients rarely hear this question, commonly asked of one lawyer by another: "Do you have client control?" If I hear this question and tell my colleague "No," I'm usually smothered with sympathy. If you ever hear one lawyer ask another, "Do you have client control?" and they're talking about you, run like hell.

A lawyer with client control can negotiate a deal and then sell it to you as if it were in your best interest. The case is resolved as the lawyer thinks it should be. This might be laudable, but I don't know any lawyers who offer to serve the time for the client because it was such a great deal.

CHAPTER 6:

Medical Marijuana & the Law

A. Current Legal Status   **92**

B. Medical Necessity   **95**

C. The Medical Referral Process   **96**
    1. *Medical Eligibility*   *97*
    2. *Confidentiality*   *98*
    3. *Finding a Medical Professional*   *100*

D. Medical Registries   **103**

E. Interacting with Police   **104**

A. CURRENT LEGAL STATUS

Since 1996, voters in several American states—California, Arizona, Nevada, Oregon, Washington, Alaska, and Maine—approved citizen-sponsored legislation legalizing the medical use of marijuana. In 2000, Hawaii's Legislature enacted a medical marijuana law. Voters in Washington, DC also approved a medical cannabis law, but political chicanery

---

California

California's Proposition 215 has been unevenly enforced depending on location. In the Northern California town of Arcata, a municipal ordinance allows patients with medical recommendations for marijuana to register with the city and receive a medical cannabis identification card which supposedly immunizes them from arrest as long as they comply with local rules. These rules include a 10 plant per patient limit. In some cases, law officers who find patients with more than ten plants seize some of the plants, leave ten intact, and charge patients with cultivation and/or cultivation for sale.

Several hundred miles south of Arcata, in the urban megalopolis of Oakland, city ordinances are extremely lenient, allowing patients to cultivate as many as 144 plants in various stages of growth, and to possess more than a pound of dried marijuana. Patients complying with these limits who provide medical documentation are immune

from arrest, as long as police find no evidence of marijuana being diverted for non-medical use.

In San Francisco, anonymous cannabis medical registration and cards are a service of the Department of Health.

In the municipalities of Oakland and Arcata, and in counties such as Mendocino and San Francisco, the spirit and the letter of Prop. 215 are being respected.

But in other California counties, such as Butte, Shasta, Glenn, Placer and Trinity County, Proposition 215 is routinely disregarded and patients continue to be arrested and prosecuted for small amounts of cannabis, regardless of the medical condition of the patients.

California legislators and the state's attorney general have attempted to draft implementing regulations to ensure 215 uniformity, but have not reached agreement on key issues.

has so far prevented this law from going into effect. On July 17, 2000 Judge Breyer ruled that medical necessity overrode federal law in the Ninth District. The U.S. Supreme Court has issued an emergency stay of this decision. Its continued validity is in question.

These new laws, along with common law medical necessity defenses, may help some cannabis users avoid being arrested for cannabis. An important caveat when considering the legal protection possibility provided by state medical cannabis laws: all of them conflict with federal law, which classifies cannabis as a "Schedule One" drug that has high potential for abuse and no legitimate medical effectiveness.

Shortly after the California initiative was approved in 1996, General Barry McCaffrey, director of the Office of National Drug Control Policy,

---

Oregon

Oregon's medical cannabis law has been more uniformly implemented. Patients who provide correct documentation and pay a $150 yearly fee receive state issued cards allowing them to possess one ounce of dried marijuana and a maximum of three plants.

The law requires an Oregon physician to state in writing that cannabis "might mitigate the symptoms of the patient's debilitating medical condition". The law defines debilitating medical conditions by providing a list of diseases and conditions. Oregon's Health Department is considering a proposal to add psychological conditions (depression, anxiety, stress disorders) to the list of approved illnesses.

"Many patients call us for help because they are having trouble with their doctors," explains John Sajo, an Oregon medical cannabis activist who heads an organization called Voter Power. "Patients have to educate their doctors that all they need do is write that medical marijuana might help. Some physicians are under the mistaken impression that they have to write a prescription. There are currently 1,000 qualified Oregon patients, and the number of people enrolled is increasing. More than 300 Oregon doctors have signed statements qualifying patients. Voter Power is now getting calls regularly from elderly patients who have never tried marijuana whose doctors are recommending it after exhausting their arsenal of pharmaceuticals."

threatened legal action against doctors who discussed medical marijuana with patients. A Federal Court placed a permanent injunction on the General and his threat was nullified. Until the July ruling, local sheriffs and prosecutors in Northern California and elsewhere referred some medical marijuana cases to federal officials, hoping to derail defendants' attempts to protect themselves with state medical cannabis laws. This still happens outside the Ninth Circuit. Some Federal judges have cooperated with medical cannabis opponents by preventing defendants from mentioning state medical cannabis laws during federal trials of medical cannabis users.

On a more positive note, federal prosecutors in several jurisdictions including Seattle, San Francisco, and Sacramento have stated or implied

---

Washington State

Washington's Initiative 692 says that a physician-approved patient may have a 60-day supply of marijuana to treat "chemotherapy-related nausea and vomiting in cancer patients; AIDS wasting syndrome; severe muscle spasms associated with multiple sclerosis and other spasticity disorders; epilepsy; acute or chronic glaucoma; and some forms of intractable pain."

I-692 does not establish any type of patient registry; it took effect December 3, 1998.

Washington's Health Department and the Legislature were supposed to fund studies and hold hearings to determine what a 60 day supply should be, but until Judge Breyer's July 17, 2000 decision in the Ninth District, *state officials claimed the federal government was preventing them from conducting studies or determining guidelines.*

The law implies patients may buy marijuana on the street and says they may grow their own or have a "caregiver" grow it for them. But it doesn't say how much a 60-day supply is, and the question of how much pot is enough has been a vexing issue for patients, police, prosecutors and courts. Washington authorities, for example, assert that medical marijuana users or caregivers must prove they aren't growing so much cannabis that they have some left over for sale or recreational use.

they will not federally prosecute marijuana defendants who would otherwise be protected by a state medical cannabis law.

The language, legal status, details, and implementation procedures of active medical marijuana laws are confusing, and are susceptible to rapidly changing interpretations and specificities as legislators, governors, public agencies, and law enforcement officials seek to modify and follow the laws' intent.

Part of the problem is that medical marijuana laws are unique on a state-by-state basis; in some cases, they are unique on an intrastate basis!

B. MEDICAL NECESSITY

There are many practical issues for marijuana users to consider when evaluating how these laws affect them. Medical cannabis users should also consider the legal doctrine called "medical necessity."

The medical necessity doctrine is based on common law and modern precedent. In an attempt to be concise, we will define "medical necessity" as the right of a person to break a law such as cannabis prohibition, in order to save life, relieve suffering, or further a greater social good. A commonly used analogy equates a husband breaking traffic laws in order to get his pregnant wife to a hospital in time for safe childbirth with a cancer patient using cannabis to mitigate the effects of chemotherapy.

Arizona

Arizona voters have voted twice on medical cannabis. They passed a medical cannabis initiative in 1996, and in 1998 they passed an initiative rejecting a legislative requirement banning physicians from prescribing cannabis until the drug receives approval from the Food and Drug Administration.

Arizona's law states that physicians may prescribe cannabis to patients when they have a second doctor's concurring opinion. Provisions of the law regarding federal prohibitions are no longer operative since it is in the Ninth Circuit.

The medical necessity defense has been victorious in criminal cases but it can be costly and time-consuming. The groundwork for such a defense must be laid down with care, timeliness, and precision before an arrest takes place. The medical necessity defense can sometimes be used to prevent arrest.

Defendants in states where there are no medical cannabis laws sometimes win acquittal, have cases dismissed or mitigated, or receive lenient sentences by proving that marijuana is the best, and perhaps the only, medicine for their severe or life-threatening condition. They must also sometimes show that the circumstances leading to their medical need for cannabis are not their own fault, and that the harm of not using cannabis was greater than the harm of using it.

C. THE MEDICAL REFERRAL PROCESS

Medical cannabis patients often find it difficult to locate credentialed medical experts who are articulate, possess knowledge of cannabis, and are willing to formally supervise or approve a patient's cannabis treatment regime.

Medical professionals involved with cannabis-using patients must be willing to provide expert testimony establishing that other medicines did not work as well as marijuana, or were harmful or ineffective. Still, prejudice and ignorance often cause juries and judges to discard expert testimony from witnesses who provide positive testimony regarding medical cannabis in favor of fallacious prosecution arguments.

Colorado

Amendment 19 was passed by Colorado voters in 1998 but derailed by a contrived signature scam initiated by the law's opponents. It passed again in 2000. A-19 allows medical patients with specific ailments to possess and cultivate small amounts of cannabis. It also protects a "primary caregiver" who provides cannabis to a patient. Amendment 19 proposes a state-sponsored, confidential registry for patients using cannabis, and protects doctors whose patients use it medicinally.

Doctors are aware that they might be harassed by law enforcement if they assist medical cannabis users. This has made it more difficult for patients who use cannabis, especially for conditions that are not overtly life threatening, such as chronic pain or depression, to find doctors who are willing to recommend it. Some medical users are discouraged by the difficulties in obtaining protection under state medical cannabis or medical necessity laws, and are frightened of revealing to medical professionals that they use cannabis. In general, however, taking advantage of the legal protections is worth the effort.

1. Medical Eligibility

Some medical cannabis proponents argue that all use is medicinal. Critics of this position argue that there are "recreational" uses of marijuana that have nothing to do with treating a diagnosed medical condition. This might be true, but it is also often the case that many cannabis users who view their use as recreational are in fact medicating themselves to alleviate conditions such as chronic pain, anxiety, attention deficit disorder or depression.

These users implicitly recognize that they feel better when they use cannabis. Such use, when evaluated by a physiologist, psychologist or psychiatrist, might be viewed as therapeutically motivated, even if the motivation is not explicit or is subconscious. Cannabis advocates and defendants should expand society's definition of medical use, especially for the purposes of using a medical defense in court.

Washington, DC

DC's Initiative 59 was sponsored by the AIDS patient coalition ACT-UP; it exempts patients from any District law prohibiting the possession or cultivation of cannabis. The initiative protects primary caregivers from criminal penalties, and sets no specific limitations on the amount patients may possess.

Initiative 59 also allows District residents to "organize not-for-profit corporations for the purpose of cultivating, purchasing, and distributing marijuana exclusively for ... medical use." The law is in limbo due to interference from Congressional Republican Bob Barr.

Nevada

In November, 2000, Nevada voters recertified "Ballot Question 9," amending the state constitution to allow patients to use cannabis legally upon the advice of their physician. The proposal also ordered the Legislature to "author-ize[e] appropriate methods for supply" of medical cannabis, and to provide for a confidential registry of patients who are authorized to use it. The measure does not specify cannabis possession or cultivation limits for patients.

In many cases, it is clear and indisputable that a person's cannabis use is "medicinal." Many users have medical conditions for which cannabis has proven or suspected medical efficacy. At present, most reputable researchers agree that marijuana is effective in mitigating chronic pain, nausea, spasticity, anorexia, glaucoma, and musculoskeletal injuries. Patients afflicted with HIV/AIDS, multiple sclerosis, Lou Gehrig's Disease and cancer patients struggling with side effects of chemotherapy all find cannabis good medicine.

Traditionally cannabis was used for many other conditions, ranging from menstrual cramps to asthma. Comprehensive pharmaceutical research currently being conducted around the world, sanctioned by governments and scientifically-accepted by peer-reviewed journals and observers, has provided preliminary results showing that cannabis is medically beneficial for some conditions.

There are some risks involved in seeking a medical cannabis recommendation.

2. Confidentiality

Many people believe that total confidentiality and trust characterize the doctor–patient relationship, but some doctors feel duty-bound to treat cannabis as a drug of abuse. It cannot automatically be assumed that physicians or nurses will have a neutral or affirming attitude toward a patient who seeks to use cannabis. In fact, patients have been busted or involuntarily committed to drug treatment programs because health care providers compromised their confidentiality. This is not likely to happen in states that have legalized medical use.

Maine

The Maine Medical Marijuana Act allows patients with a doctor's recommendation to use cannabis. If arrested by state or local authorities on marijuana charges, a qualified patient or "caregiver" can claim immunity from prosecution under state law if she or he is using the cannabis for certain medical purposes.

In order to use marijuana as medicine, a patient must be diagnosed by a physician as suffering from one or more of the following conditions:

1. Persistent nausea, vomiting, wasting syndrome or loss of appetite as a result of AIDS or the treatment thereof or chemotherapy or radiation therapy used to treat cancer;

2. Heightened intraocular pressure as a result of glaucoma;

3. Seizures associated with a chronic, debilitating disease, such as epilepsy;

4. Persistent muscle spasms associated with chronic, debilitating disease, such as multiple sclerosis.

Note that a physician must state that cannabis is appropriate for treatment of a specific illness or symptom. Simply having a qualifying disease does not automatically qualify anyone for protection under the Maine Medical Marijuana Act.

The Act specifies that doctors and patients must have a bona fide physician-patient relationship. Doctors must: 1) discuss with the patient the risks and benefits of the medical use of cannabis, 2) give her/his opinion of the balance of risks and benefits for this person, 3) advise the patient that they might benefit from medical use of cannabis, and 4) provide continuing care for the patient.

Proof that these four steps have been carried out, along with the patient's diagnosis, should be documented in the patient's medical record. In addition, the doctor must provide an authenticated copy of the medical record or other written documentation to her/his patient indicating that the patient has a covered illness and that in the doctor's opinion, the benefits of cannabis would outweigh the risks.

The Act protects doctors who follow these guidelines from any negative professional or legal consequences. None of the steps involved in helping a patient get cannabis authorization expose a physician to threatened punishments like revocation of prescription licenses, cutoff from Medicare and Medicaid eligibility, or

---

Maine (*continued*)

criminal prosecution. Experts in medical law were consulted when the law was drafted.

After discussing cannabis with their doctors as outlined above, patients should ask the doctor for an authenticated (certified) copy of their medical record or written documentation indicating that they have a medical marijuana recommendation. This will be the basis for their protection under the Act. Patients should make copies and keep at least one in a secure place; they should also try to have one with them or with any marijuana they possess.

Under the Maine Medical Marijuana Act, the allowable amount of cannabis for medical use is 1 ¼ ounces or less of harvested marijuana. It also permits eligible patients to cultivate a total of 6 plants, of which not more than 3 may be mature, flowering plants. If a patient has more than the permitted amount, even if they have their doctor's recommendation, they are in violation of the law and subject to prosecution.

The Act recognizes that some patients may be in such ill health that a family member or close friend may need to possess marijuana for that patient. Therefore, "designated caregivers" are allowed to help the patient and are also exempted from marijuana charges as long as they abide all aspects of the law.

The Act defines a "designated caregiver" as someone who has consistently assumed responsibility for a person's housing, health, or safety. This person must be so designated in writing by the patient, or have been granted power of attorney for the health care of the patient.

---

3. Finding a Medical Professional

How can a person find a health care provider sympathetic to medical cannabis use? In states where voters have legalized medical cannabis, there are usually cannabis buyers' cooperatives, patients' associations, cannabis lobbying groups, and other networking or affinity groups that guide people toward cannabis-friendly health providers. Word-of-mouth referrals are useful; other patients and caregivers may know of doctors who are willing to assist patients who require medical cannabis. Internet chat rooms are safe places for patients seeking doctor information. National groups, such as Americans for Medical Rights, Marijuana

Policy Project, and the Alliance for Cannabis Therapeutics, may also provide assistance. Many doctors have no opinion on medical cannabis; they need to be vetted and educated. If unsure of a doctor's attitude, a patient may phrase their interest as an innocent query; rather than saying, "I use medical pot." A patient could say, "I have heard that cannabis may be helpful for my condition, what do you think?" Patients have the right to expect privacy, and might mention the confidentiality issue.

A health professional concerned about a patient's welfare should be open-minded about medical cannabis. A patient could offer to provide medical literature, research citations or other scholarly information that help professionals understand cannabis's usefulness. Doctors may propose that patients take Marinol®, which is a prescription pill that contains synthetic THC.

Marinol® is usually far less effective than whole cannabis, with a slower relief onset and more negative side effects. It is also very expensive. But it is prudent to accept such a prescription, and to fill it at least once. If a patient is arrested or questioned by police, a Marinol® prescription can help to defeat the usefulness of urine testing (which is often required for people on bail, pre-trial release, or awaiting sentencing). A Marinol® prescription is also a tool that may force jail or prison officials to provide THC to an incarcerated patient.

Hawaii

Hawaii's medical cannabis law, passed in April, stipulates that patients with recommendations can grow a maximum of six plants. The Honolulu Police Department fought the bill, and warned that marijuana use was prohibited under federal law and that the state law would technically not shield licensed users from federal prosecution. Since the Ninth Circuit decision and Supreme Court action, this is in question.

The bill allows victims of AIDS, cancer patients undergoing chemotherapy, and people with glaucoma and epilepsy to use and grow cannabis. Patients must register with police agencies.

If a patient is confident that there is more good than harm in talking to their doctor about cannabis, the patient should be prepared to present a detailed description of his or her illness and symptoms, especially as it relates to medical cannabis use.

Ideally, a physician who writes a medical marijuana recommendation should be one who specializes in the field of medicine most relevant to a patient's illness. Some courts and police officers have rejected recommendations written by psychiatrists, for example, when the patient's condition was a physical illness, such as multiple sclerosis. Find a doctor who specializes in the ailment for which you seek medical cannabis.

Pete Brady:

I underwent back surgery; the surgery failed. My spine began deteriorating rapidly. The symptoms of my injury were chronic severe pain, loss of sensation, nerve damage, muscle spasms, soft tissue inflammation, and depression. Doctors prescribed huge amounts of prescription narcotics, which had severe side effects.

Cannabis countered many of my symptoms and also alleviated some of the underlying causes of my disease. It relaxed my muscles, reduced swelling and pain, and lifted my mood. Marijuana's effectiveness helped me kick the drugs prescribed for my condition. Monitoring my cannabis usage by keeping track of dosage amounts, ancillary effects, and the different medical properties of individual marijuana strains was helpful. I began breeding strains that produced the desired medical effects. I also experimented with eating cannabis versus smoking it. I kept careful notes. I also engaged in physical rehabilitation and other treatments while using it. By taking responsibility for my own health, and pursuing every recovery option available, I showed that I was indeed a medical patient, rather than somebody who just liked to smoke pot but also had a medical condition that benefited from cannabis.

When I told my HMO physician about my cannabis use, he did not endorse or condemn it. I contacted a physician affiliated with a medical cannabis cooperative, provided him my medical records, and received his written authorization to use cannabis medically.

D. MEDICAL REGISTRIES

Some localities have instituted registry systems, which issue identification cards or other materials that identify legal medical cannabis patients. In some places, such as Oregon, municipal, county and state health officials facilitate such registration. In Oakland, California, a private medical cannabis club provides a registry service for the city. Public and private registries usually require periodic recertifications, and often charge fees, but these hassles are a small price to pay for the protection afforded by having official certification as a medical cannabis patient.

The underlying benefit of registry systems is that law enforcement officials may choose to walk away from a contact with a medical cannabis user who is registered. The situation may become much more complicated, however, if medical cultivation or a caregiver/provider is involved. Police almost always assume that cannabis cultivation is for commercial purposes. The fewer plants or dried herb a patient has, the better. One well-trimmed, bushy plant can produce as much medicine as several single-stalk plants. Unless a patient is in a locality that specifies how many plants or how much marijuana can be legally possessed, the best policy is to have the least amount possible. Be careful to document the legitimacy of a caregiver relationship, especially if the caregiver is not a medical user but merely a provider and/or grower.

It is also important for medical users to avoid all trappings of "recreational" use or sales. Police have cited innocent items, such as sandwich bags, cash, and bathroom scales as evidence to support felony sales charges. In all but the most progressive locales, patients should assume that if police can contrive a reason to make a cannabis arrest, they will. Don't give them any ammunition.

It must be noted that many medical cannabis advocates reject the registry paradigm. They say that patients should not have to give up their right to privacy or provide police with information that could later be used against them. These suspicions are similar to those voiced by gun owners, who fear that if registration of all firearms becomes mandatory, a tyrannical government might use the registry as an easy way of finding armed citizens. Merely registering a marijuana user or garden does not give absolute protection in some localities. Police may still visit the home of a registered cannabis patient; they may still arrest a registered medical cannabis user on suspicion of sales or distribution. Sometimes, even calling the authorities to ask questions about local regulations or registries can result in a visit from the cops. While inquiring about one's rights cannot be used to obtain a warrant or otherwise implicate a person, all it takes is the "odor" of cannabis that the cop supposedly smells when you open your door to lead to a warrant, and if anything is found, to result in an arrest. After decades of police abuses, many citizens are understandably reluctant to provide the address of a medical cannabis user and garden. That being said, this author could find no evidence that participating in a registry has increased or lowered chance of arrest.

E. INTERACTING WITH POLICE

If the worst happens, and a law enforcement officer questions a patient about marijuana, he or she has to decide whether to selectively give up the "right to remain silent" or to say nothing to an officer until a lawyer is present. In states without medical cannabis laws, there may or may not be any advantage in speaking to an officer, and there may be much to lose. The medical necessity defense is usually only found to be useful

---

Your State's Laws

Medical marijuana databanks contain information indicating that the following states may have active laws that set up marijuana research programs or at least partially recognize marijuana's medical efficacy. These states include Connecticut, Georgia, Iowa, Louisiana, Massachusetts, Minnesota, Montana, Missouri, New Hampshire, North Dakota, New Jersey, New Mexico, New York, North Carolina, Ohio, South Carolina, Rhode Island, Tennessee, Texas, Vermont, Virginia, West Virginia, and Wisconsin.

More information about these laws can be found on the Internet. Some resources to begin your search with appear in Appendix.

after an arrest, as an affirmative defense. A police officer can still arrest you. Still in some cases, medical necessity could deter a conviction. Remember that when police officers say, "Everything you say can and will be used against you in a court of law," they mean that even the most innocent statement will probably be twisted or misinterpreted to your disadvantage.

Documentation of Medical Authorization to Possess Marijuana
for Medical Purposes

*Patient Name:*_____

*Date of Birth:*_____

I am a physician licensed in the state of _____.
I am treating the above named patient for one or more of the specified
debilitating conditions: _____

_____

_____

_____.

I have advised the above named patient about potential risks and benefits
of the medical use of marijuana. I have assessed the above named patient's
medical history and medical condition. It is my medical opinion that the

potential benefits of the medical use of marijuana would likely outweigh
the health risks for this patient.

*Signature of Physician:*_____

*Printed Name of Physician:*_____

*Date:*_____

In states with medical cannabis laws, a patient may be able to prevent arrest by providing a recent recommendation from a doctor along with other registry certification if available. Patients should immediately present registry cards or other documents proving the patient is a bona fide medical cannabis user. Some people post copies of relevant documents and medical notices on their walls, in areas where they store cannabis, and/or next to any cannabis plants they are cultivating.

Patients should not engage in dialogue with officers beyond this brief statement: "I am a medical cannabis user exempt from prosecution and arrest. I have documentation from my doctor (and/or from a state-approved medical cannabis registry) proving that my use is legal. Please examine it. Please do not endanger my life by arresting me or seizing my medicine." In some circumstances, it may be advisable to have an officer contact a patient's health professional or the registry that has certified a patient.

Patients should use discretion in discussing cannabis use with police officers. Explaining medical conditions and how cannabis helps may not be detrimental; however, discussion about how you procure or supply medical cannabis, or the amount of cannabis used are usually counterproductive. Just present documentation and insist that officers respect medical need. Do not consent to searches, or make statements. If you are arrested, inform every arresting officer, court official, jail supervisor, and other government employee that you are a medical user, that your arrest is unjustified, and that arrest and incarceration are detrimental to your health.

Anyone wishing to utilize medical cannabis should seek up-to-date and locally applicable legal information in addition to medical information at the outset of their use to best prepare and protect themselves in the event that law enforcement intervenes. Some helpful resources are provided in the appendix.

CHAPTER 7:

Drug Testing

**A. The Rise of Workplace
Drug Testing**   **108**

B. Workplace Testing Laws   **110**
   1. Who Can Test?   110
   2. What Can I Be Tested For?   112
   3. When Can I Be Tested?   113
     a. Pre-employment   114
     b. Reasonable Suspicion   114
     c. Post-Accident/Post-Injury   115
     d. Return-to-Duty/Post-Treatment   115
     e. Random   115
   4. Where Can I Be Tested?   116

C. Types of Drug Tests   **118**
   1. All Tests Are Not Created Equal   118
   2. Urine Tests   120
   3. Hair Tests   123
   4. Blood Tests   125
   5. Tests in Development   125
     a. Saliva Tests   125
     b. Perspiration Tests   126

D. Passing and Failing   **127**
   1. Cleaning Out   128
   2. Committing Adulteration or Substitution   131
   3. False Positives   133

E. Recourse   **134**

F. The Politics of Drug Testing   **137**

A. THE RISE OF WORKPLACE DRUG TESTING

If you have looked for employment in the last decade, you have probably been asked to submit to a drug test. Although drug screening is used throughout the legal system—for example, as a condition of parole—people who have had no encounters with law enforcement are most likely to be introduced to drug testing in the workplace.

A study by the American Management Association revealed that in 1987, less than a quarter of its corporate members had implemented drug testing, but by 1996, over three quarters of these members were testing. Statistics from the Drug and Alcohol Testing Industry Association state that 95 percent of Fortune 500 companies test for drugs. In 1997, more than 40 million American workers were tested for drugs related to their potential or continued employment.

Rates of drug testing in the workplace continue to rise. Some private businesses are mandated by law to test their employees; most notably, companies in the transportation industries such as aviation, railroad, interstate motor carriers, or mass transit. Most private employers are not required to test by law, but have decided to use drug testing programs based on claims that such testing benefits the company in terms of efficiency, productivity, and financial gain. Another reason for testing is the general acceptance of the Drug War campaign.

The problem is most businesses are getting the bulk of their information about the specific benefits and downsides of drug testing from the burgeoning drug testing industry itself, which has an obvious vested interest. Drug testing has become a $1-1/2 billion industry in the United States.

Drug War logic encourages companies to adopt drug-testing programs on claims that drug users:

> are less productive,
> are absent more frequently,
> cost more in health care benefits,
> have more accidents, and
> file more compensation claims.

Screening for drugs allows companies to feel they are doing their part to filter out a potential detriment to their company. Most employers are not experts on drug use or abuse. Many companies have merely jumped on the drug testing bandwagon based on the prevalence of drug testing by other employers. Personal or organizational morals, or unscientific assumptions may serve as the basis for deciding to drug test.

FEDERAL DRUG TESTING LEGISLATION

Workplace drug testing is relatively new, dating back to federal legislation that took effect in 1988. The Drug-Free Workplace Act (HR-5210-124 Section 5152 [1988]), enacted under the Reagan administration, was the first federal legislation that mandated drug testing. While this Act pertained only to certain government employees, it has laid the groundwork for most of the current workplace drug-testing regulations and procedures.

Under President Bush, The Omnibus Transportation Employee Testing Act of 1991 furthered the 1988 Act, turning existing regulations for the Department of Transportation into federal law (49 CFR Part 40). The Omnibus Act expanded mandated drug testing under federal law. It also expanded the list of drugs tested for to include alcohol, which had been overlooked in the original legislation.

These two laws introduced

mandatory drug testing in an incremental fashion, requiring all military and safety-sensitive government employees to undergo drug testing. All employers in the transportation industry followed, and then anyone who contracted work with the government in the amount of $25,000 per year or more were required to comply. This last category introduced mandatory testing to private industry as a condition of working with the government.

After the introduction of law for testing of government employees, many private businesses followed suit. Since the early 1990s, workplace testing has grown exponentially. The drug testing industry has flourished as a result of the increased demand, and has become a major industry in the U.S. As a result, this legislation has created a new front on which the War on Drugs is being waged.

Once they implement a program for drug testing, companies often investigate no further. The overwhelming majority of employers who implement drug testing are not collecting or analyzing data to see if it makes any difference in workplace efficiency, productivity, or financial gain.

According to the American Management Association (AMA) 1996 survey, less than 10 percent of companies with drug testing programs had performed *any* cost benefit analysis. None had strong statistical correlations showing declines in absenteeism, accident rates, disability claims, or rates of employee theft or violence as a result of instituting drug-testing measures. A 1999 review of drug testing studies by the American Civil Liberties Union (ACLU) also showed no clear relationships between the factors listed above and the presence or absence of a drug-testing program.

Many people, civil rights organizations, and worker's rights organizations oppose drug testing as an intrusion on civil liberties that are granted by the constitution. Drug testing is a legal issue, and it is important to know your rights when you are faced with a drug test. A drug test is also a scientific procedure whereby a sample is taken and tested for the presence of certain drugs or their metabolites. It is helpful to know the basics of how drug tests work so you can assess your risk when submitting to a test.

B. WORKPLACE TESTING LAWS

In the last section, we considered some of the possible answers to why you may be subject to drug testing in the workplace. In considering the law, the questions of who, what, when, and where are important. After that we will turn to the question of how, addressing the basic science involved in drug testing methods.

1. Who Can Test?

Any workplace can implement a drug-testing program, but the rules are different depending on whether the workplace is public or private.

Federal guidelines apply only to government workers, businesses with government contracts over a certain monetary amount per year, and safety-sensitive workers in public and private industry. Private industry is only subject to government guidelines insofar as they fall under federal requirements for government contractors or safety-sensitive employees. The guarantees of the Fourth Amendment to the Constitution, which protects against unreasonable searches and seizures, offers its citizens this protection from the government, and this extends to the government as an employer. It says nothing about protecting you from private businesses. Rules and procedures for the what, when, where, and why of drug testing have been outlined and approved by Congress and/or states in order to keep drug testing by the government from crossing the boundary of the protections given in the Constitution. Some would argue that drug testing crosses that line, or at least verges on its edges. Many states have further requirements for public employers who adopt and administer a workplace drug-testing program.

The rules and rights are different if you are an employee in private industry. In the world of private industry, anything goes. While there are possible legal ramifications for a company that tests unfairly, there are no guidelines set by the federal government that limit private industry testing policy. The protections of the Constitution, such as the Fourth Amendment right against unreasonable search and seizure, do not apply to private industry, and will not assist in litigation against unfair testing.

Private industry can test using the method of their choice for the illicit substances of their choice at the time that they choose to do so. The only recourse to an unfair policy is in taking the company to court, and this can be costly and risky. Companies with unions may have collective bargaining agreements that allow the employees some determination in the drug-testing policy of their workplace.

Some companies may use outdated methods of testing or non-certified labs for processing. Many, but not all, companies, on advise of their legal counsel, will follow a standard testing procedure derived from the federal government's guidelines for federally mandated testing in order to protect themselves from litigation.

At one Fortune 500 company, 59 percent of the employees who tested positive for drugs tested positive for marijuana. A positive result for marijuana only indicates that the employee who tested positive smoked marijuana days or weeks earlier.

Drug testing is simply not a cost-effective business practice. To test 100 employees using an immunoassay is around $10 per employee. The GC/MS confirmation test for any positive immunoassay results is around $100 not including any administrative or overhead expenses. Overall, the rate of positive tests is 5 percent. Of these, approximately 3 percent test positive for cannabinoids. The company has spent thousands of dollars to discover that 5 of their employees did drugs at some time in the recent past. Of these 5 in 100, 3 of them smoked marijuana.

A recent study by the U. S. Postal Service that tracked over 4,000 new employees revealed no significant difference in the success rates of employees who tested positive versus those who tested clean.

2. What Can I Be Tested For?

Employers who must comply with federal regulations are required to test for alcohol and five controlled substances:

- Cannabinoids: marijuana, hashish
- Cocaine: cocaine, crack, benzoylecognine
- Amphetamines: speed, amphetamines, methamphetamines
- Opiates: opium, heroin, codeine, morphine
- Phencyclidine: PCP/angel dust

These five drugs are typically referred to as the NIDA-5 or the DHHS-5, named for the organizations responsible for setting forth the regulations: the National Institute of Drug Abuse and the Department of Heath and Human Safety, respectively.

The American Disabilities Act (ADA) is a federal law that also includes a restriction on what can be tested for, because it limits medical inquiries by employers. The ADA provides the groundwork for a legal claim if a non-safety employee qualifying under the disabilities act is disciplined for a positive test on a substance other than the five standard substances listed above.

State laws may also limit or expand what substances can or must be tested in correlation with the requirements given by federal law. For instance, Iowa permits but does not require testing for drugs beyond the NIDA-5. Minnesota state law limits the conditions under which workplace drug and alcohol testing can be conducted. Ohio, on the other hand, provides financial incentives for workplace programs to test beyond the NIDA-5, and state programs such as the Ohio Bureau of Workers Compensation Drug-Free Workplace program requires testing for nine drugs.

Workplaces where unions engage in a collective bargaining process may have some employee input on how workplace drug testing is conducted in private industry. Private industry without union representation is open to setting policy with few if any regulations or restrictions for what they test for, or what method is used.

3. When Can I Be Tested?

Legally, government employers are within their rights if they can show a rational cause for testing. This is not the same as probable cause. The difference between rational cause and probable cause may seem tedious, but the distinction is important. Probable cause is more rigorous, requiring an action to be based most probably on the cause that was suspected. The appropriate question for probable cause: "was the reason correct?" Rational cause only means that there is an articulable, logical reason for taking an action, even though there could have been many other possible causes. With rational cause, the reason doesn't have to be the most likely, just possible. The appropriate question for rational cause: "was there any reason that makes sense whatsoever?"

Drug use may not be the probable cause for a person yawning excessively at work every Monday; that is, drugs are not the most likely cause. Many things could be the cause. But drug use is one rational explanation—which means it's reason enough to get you drug tested, and stand up in a court of law. If you think that's bad, remember that private businesses do not even have to show a rational cause to test you.

Federal guidelines indicate that testing is allowable at five possible times. To be fair, most private businesses, on advice of their lawyers, also stick to these five possible times in order to avoid any potential lawsuits, but this is only a yardstick rather than a requirement.

a. Pre-employment

This is the one that most people probably think of and dread as the big hurdle. It is also the most commonly conducted testing for non-safety, private positions of employment. Previous to being employed, a prospective employee may be required to pass a drug test as a condition of being hired. This type of testing is almost always upheld by courts in that an applicant voluntarily chooses to seek employment in a certain profession and is not compelled to continue with the application if they find the company's drug-testing policy offensive. Courts have held that those who voluntarily chose to accept a job that requires drug testing have a lower expectation of privacy. Recourse for pre-employment drug testing is practically nonexistent, but there are things you can do at the time of testing, which will be discussed later.

b. Reasonable Suspicion

A drug test based on "reasonable suspicion" should be conducted "under circumstances exhibiting individualized suspicion of on-the-job impairment and with evidence of substantial reliability." The following factors have been described by the courts as acceptable bases for reasonable suspicion testing:

- Direct observation of an employee either engaged in drug-related activity or exhibiting physical symptoms of being under the influence of a drug
- Indirect information regarding an employee engaging in such activities provided by a credible source or corroborated independently
- A sudden and inexplicable change in the performance of work, or in the rate of tardiness or absenteeism, or an increase in instances of negligence
- A conviction or arrest for an offense which is related to drugs, or an ongoing criminal investigation of an employee for illicit drug use, possession, or trafficking

- Evidence that the employee tampered with the drug test
- The development of abnormal or erratic behavior patterns

c. Post-Accident/Post-Injury

For employees in the transportation industries, a drug test will follow an accident. Outside of these industries, it is likely that a drug test will follow an injury of any kind while on the job. It does not matter if the accident was someone else's fault, or classified as a "no-fault" accident: you can still be required to submit to a drug test as a matter of course. The same is true of an injury. Whether the injury was "no-fault" or you were injured directly or not, your presence or interaction with the worker injured at the site of the injury may be enough to require you to submit to testing.

d. Return-to-Duty/ Post-Treatment

Return-to-duty testing may offer the employee a second chance when they have had a previous positive test. When testing positive or admitting to previous use—if not fired as a result—an employee will enter the system of referral, which they must negotiate in order to be able to return to their job. This may involve going through a drug treatment program, or meeting with health professionals. An almost-guaranteed part of this process is return-to-duty testing. The policy for allowing positive testers to return to duty differs among government employers and from state to state, to say nothing of the variance in policy in private industry.

e. Random

Among public employees, random testing is only allowable for safety-sensitive positions. Random means that there is an equal chance for any employee working that day to be subject to a test, and random selection may be determined through a computer program designed for government safety-sensitive sectors for this purpose. Non-safety government positions are not subject to random testing. However, private employers can randomly test their employees—or not so randomly test their employees—as they see fit.

4. Where Can I Be Tested?

While the sample may be collected on site, there are some rules for federal employees that apply to sample collection. Federal rules do not allow instant on-site test kits to be used. Some states require that the sample be collected by a licensed medical professional (Minnesota is one such state). Federal regulations require that the sample collector be trained. Private employers may use instant, on-site tests if they choose, although some states have adopted rules that require even non-regulated employers to use only trained collectors. Many but not all private companies may choose to conduct testing collection and analysis through outside professionals on advice of legal counsel because this removes direct liability for mistaken results—and potential resulting lawsuits—outside of the company.

Urine samples are usually collected under controlled circumstances. This often requires the employee to go to a facility designed for collection, where sample collection is "supervised;" that is, someone else is present with you while you take a whiz to make sure you don't try to tamper with the test or substitute your sample with anything else. The sink in the restroom used for sample collection may have the water turned off, and the toilet water may even be colored blue to keep all test subjects from using this water to dilute a sample.

If you are an employee subject to federal guidelines, the path your sample takes after being submitted is also quite elaborate and defined. Federal rule and many state laws require that the sample be analyzed by a laboratory certified through the DHHS, the College of American Pathology (CAP) or possibly another certifying agency. Private employers do not have to use certified labs to analyze the sample; if they use an outside source rather than in-house or instant testing, they may choose any agency that advertises to do this type of work.

A certified lab may sound official, and it is true that the controls and accuracy of these labs are much higher than uncertified labs, and the documentation procedures are extensive. The unfortunate truth of the matter, however, is that there is no system in place to hold these labs accountable for meeting the standards required for certification. A certified lab must submit to lab testing, whereby they run a known sample through their analysis procedure and should come up with the correct percentages for this sample. They then submit the results to the certifying agency, and the agency confirms that they are measuring the known sample at numbers within an acceptable degree of accuracy. However, at this point in time, if a certified lab fails to meet these standards, there is no administrative recourse. When they are given a sample and fail to show the readings within an acceptable margin of error, they submit their results, the certification lab tells them that they failed and—nothing. Nothing happens as a matter of policy. They continue operating and are left to their own internal business procedures to make any changes leading to compliance, but there is no incentive built into the review to encourage them to comply.

According to a 1994 book by the National Research Council Committee on Drug Use in the Workplace, there are 3 important distinctions when considering the application of drug testing laws:

1. PUBLIC OR PRIVATE
Drug testing by any government employer or by private industry that must comply with federal government mandates are under much more strict regulation than private industries that adopt a voluntary drug testing program. There is also a stronger basis for legal recourse because the constitution protects its citizens from unreasonable search and seizure by government agents and limits government searches to those that can show cause in accordance with the Fourth Amendment to the Constitution. It does not offer such protections from private individuals or organizations if they are not acting according to a mandate of the government.

2. PRE-EMPLOYMENT OR POST-EMPLOYMENT
Generally, both public and private workplaces are granted more liberty in testing people not yet employed than persons already employed by their company.

3. FEDERAL OR STATE
Employees of the government are protected by federal law. State law does not interfere or prevent testing of federal government employees in conformity with federal law. However, testing with no regulation by or protection from the federal government may be controlled by particular states' laws.

This can be an important factor to keep in mind if you contest the results of any drug test. Certified labs may not be as monolithically efficient as they would have you believe. While the lab's equipment may be capable of a high degree of accuracy, human error at setting calibration, or in any administrative step in the testing process is overwhelmingly responsible for inaccurate results.

C. TYPES OF DRUG TESTS

1. All Tests Are Not Created Equal

Drug tests are designed to pinpoint certain substances that a person has ingested. These tests measure the metabolites in the system using several chemical processes. When a drug is ingested, the body breaks it down and metabolizes the drug, much like how the body digests and metabolizes food. This metabolized form of the drug is measured through a sample from the individual, such as blood or urine. But all drug tests do not test for all drugs, nor do they test equally.

The metabolite of the active ingredient in marijuana, THC, lodges in the fatty tissues of the body. These metabolites remain in the fatty tissue long after the effects of marijuana have worn off. The presence of these metabolites is used to prove that the subject recently consumed marijuana. Marijuana is the most common substance for which people test positive, at least in part because marijuana metabolites stay in the system longer than most other drugs. Because they stay in the body longer, a test may come back positive even if an individual smoked marijuana days or even months before the test. Since rate of metabolism and rate of marijuana use vary for every individual, and a number of other lifestyle choices can come into play, there is no generically applicable figure for how long metabolites remain in the body. Everyone is different.

Several types of tests have been developed to detect drugs and drug metabolites. These tests differ in what they use as a sample, and in the scientific method of detection. Urine, hair, and blood are the three most common samples, although there are attempts to develop tests based on perspiration and saliva as well. At this time, urine testing is the most common sample requested for testing. Urine testing is the sample method required by federal guidelines.

There are also several scientific methods that are used to detect the presence of drug metabolites. Finally, tests vary in the substances for

---

Beyond the NIDA-5:
Substances That May Be Tested For in a Drug Test

Federal regulations, determined by the National Institute on Drug Abuse (NIDA) and the Substance Abuse and Mental Health Services Administration (SAMHSA), a branch of the Department of Health and Human Services (DHHS), require companies that fall under federal guidelines to test for five specific categories of drugs. These are sometimes called the "NIDA-5" or "DHHS-5." Testing for these five substances plus alcohol is mandatory for those falling under federal guidelines. Many drug testing policies that are not federally mandated will still be focused around these same five substances, although state requirements and private companies not subject to federal guidelines may vary from this standard.
The NIDA-5 are:
- **Cannabinoids:** *marijuana, hashish*
- **Cocaine:** *cocaine, crack, benzoylecognine*
- **Amphetamines:** *speed, methamphetamines*

- **Opiates:** *opium, heroin, codeine, morphine*
- **Phencyclidine:** *PCP/angel dust*
An expanded test may include the above along with a combination of:
- *Barbiturates: Phenobarbital, Secobarbital, Butabital*
- *Methaqualone: Quaaludes*
- *Benzodiazepines: valium, Librium, serax, rohypnol*
- *Methadone*
- *Propoxyphene: darvon compounds*
- *Ethanol*
Most companies will not include all 6 of the above categories in an expanded drug test, but may add any combination of 2–4 of the above. A few other substances are only occasionally tested for; such testing is currently unusual. These substances include:
- *LSD: acid*
- *Hallucinogens: psilocybin mushrooms, MDMA, MDA, MDE, mescaline*
- *Inhalants: toluene, xylene, benzene*

which they are screening. The choice of what drugs to screen for may be based on company policy, federal regulation requirements, and expense of the test. All companies subject to federal regulations test for marijuana use; most companies that test using urine as a sample test for marijuana.

2. Urine Tests

Urine testing is the cheapest type of testing, is less controversial than hair testing, and is less intrusive than blood testing. Among urine tests, there are a few different screening processes. A common standard is to first screen samples through an immunoassay test, then confirm positive immunoassay tests through a second test with the more accurate gas chromatograph mass spectrometer (GC/MS). While this procedure is the standard, the second test is not always performed. Occasionally, only the GC/MS is used, but it is significantly more expensive to use. Regulations under SAMSHA and NIDA, and the Dept. of Defense guidelines currently accept only an immunoassay followed by a CG/MS confirmation as the proper drug testing procedure.

In the past, the Thin Layer Chromatography (TLC) test was commonly used, but this test is now considered technologically obsolete. Compared with the immunoassay and the GC/MS tests, the TLC has a low level of accuracy, and offers less information. The TLC can only give yes–no information about the presence or absence of a substance, whereas the GC/MS test measures the amount present. It is improbable, but not impossible that any drug test you would take would be the Thin Layer Chromatography. It is *more* likely that you have heard word-of-mouth information on how to pass a drug test that was true for passing the TLC, but won't work with the newer tests.

Drug tests are serious biochemistry. During an immunoassay test, the urine sample is combined with a "tagged drug," and an antibody that the drug you are being tested for binds to. If the drug metabolite is in the urine, it binds to the antibody. The "tagged drug," which the lab can identify and distinguish from any drug metabolites in the urine, also tries to bind to the antibody. The more drug metabolite present in the urine, the less the "tagged drug" can attach to the antibody. Immunoassay tests compare the test results with a sample containing a known amount of a drug. They use this to determine whether the test urine contained a measurable amount of the substance it was attempting to detect. There are three different methods of immunoassay testing. Antibodies can be detected through enzymes (EMIT), radioisotopes

Confirming the Confirmation Test

The procedure specified in federal regulation guidelines mandates companies under its direction to use an immunoassay as the screening test, and confirm any positive immunoassay results with a gas chromatography/mass spectrometry (GC/MS) test.

The GC/MS test is more rigorous and gives results in a percentage that is in the units nanogram per milliliter. Consider that a nanogram per milliliter is like finding a red golf ball in a gymnasium filled to the ceiling with golf balls. While the sample is pretty small, this test measures very slight amounts of very tiny units, making for a precise measurement when the machinery is calibrated correctly.

While this is the prescribed method, the GC/MS is a much more expensive test—it can cost $100 per sample as opposed to the approximately $10 per sample that an immunoassay costs.

Administrative errors, such as a failure to divide the initial sample before running an immunoassay test, can make the second test impossible without collecting another sample. Given these factors, it is important to follow up any positive result with a request for the test results. If the organization that tested you cannot provide a ng/mL result, they did not follow the immunoassay test with a confirmation test. If you are a public employee, they have broken the required protocol for testing, and they are lying. This can work strongly in your favor.

Keep in mind that only federal and some state employees fall under guidelines that mandate this confirmatory test by law. In other sectors, this is not a required procedure, but is an accepted standard. The information may still be useful for contesting results, and could be useful if they lied to you about them. It is less useful as a legal defense, because the laws do not regulate testing, nor are they designed to protect you from private business practices in the way that they are intended to protect you from unjust government practices.

(RIA), or fluorescent compounds (FPIA). The advantages of the immunoassay method are that it is a relatively cheap test ($8–12 per screen test if bought in volume)and it allows very small amounts of a drug to be detected in a small amount of urine. One disadvantage is that it may not be able to specifically identify a drug within a class of drugs because the drug–antibody combination would be too similar to distinguish the difference between other substances in the same drug family.

The GC/MS may be the only test used, or may be the test used to confirm positive test results from an immunoassay screening. GC/MS, or

The EMIT, or Enzyme Multiple Immunoassay Test, is the cheapest, most common, and the easiest to process of the immunoassay tests. Often, private companies use EMIT as the first screening for a pre-employment drug test, but there is no standardized procedure for drug testing in private companies. EMIT is a very common test used because it is cheap and widely available. Even the company that manufactures EMIT admits that it expects about 10 percent of tests to come back with false positives.

The RIA or Radio Immunoassay test is based on the same principle as the EMIT—the interaction with antibodies—but uses radioactive iodine as the way of detecting the antibodies, rather than an enzyme. Compared with EMIT, the RIA test is a little more sensitive, making it harder to pass. The U.S. government, including the military, currently uses the RIA test. The EMIT is more commonly used by private industry because the RIA produces radioactive waste, which can be tricky to deal with for private businesses.

The FPIA, or Fluorescence Polarization Immunoassay test, like the EMIT and RIA, uses the same method but instead detects by measuring the activity of a molecule when it is exposed to plane polarized light. It is more expensive and more sensitive, especially in identifying amphetamines. Because of its greater expense, FPIA is only occasionally used as the first screening test. Sometimes FPIA is used as a second screening test. If another immunoassay was used as the initial screen, the FPIA cannot be used as a confirmatory test by the government because guidelines require the confirmation test to use a different chemical principle than the initial screen.

gas chromatography/mass spectrometry is a two-step procedure. The GC, or gas chromatography process, separates the sample into its constituent parts through heating the sample to vaporize it. The MS or mass spectrometry process of the test is the analysis of the separated sample. Mass spectrometry bombards each compound with electrons, which makes it fragment into a characteristic and reproducible molecular pattern, or what some call its "molecular fingerprint." GC/MS is precise, definitive, and has a low number of false results that are mostly due to "human error." It is also a costly process. Statistics on GC/MS quote it at a 99 percent accuracy level. When you consider that the number of drug tests given each year are now in the millions, one percent inaccuracy means that for every million tested, ten thousand results are wrong. Still, the chances of fooling this test are much lower and more limited.

Immunoassay offers yes–no information about the presence of a drug. GC/MS tests measure the presence of drugs in terms of the drugs concentration in the sample (nanograms per milliliter). The generally accepted screening cutoff for marijuana is 100 nanograms/ milliliter (ng/mL). The standard cutoff for the Dept. of Transportation is 50 ng/mL. Some tests can be as low as 15 ng/mL.

3. Hair Tests

Testing the hair for the presence of illicit substances was proven possible as early as the 1950s. Most research on the ability to drug test using hair as a sample has taken place since 1970, and has become more intense as the Drug War climate has increased the interest in developing drug-testing techniques. Hair testing remains a fledgling technology.

To conduct a drug test using a hair sample, hair can be taken from any part of the body and is typically about the diameter of a pencil and 1.5 inches long. A test cannot be performed on one strand of hair. Hair testing is supposed to be capable of detecting drug use for months, or however long one's hair has been growing. While urinalysis tends to be disadvantageous to marijuana users, the sensitivity of hair testing for marijuana is not well established. Not all employers who drug test with hair samples screen for marijuana. This type of testing is more sensitive to cocaine.

Hair tests are not affected by short-term abstinence from drugs. Hair can sometimes be used to determine when certain substances were used and that their use has been continued, but drugs such as cocaine tend to "travel" on the hair, making time period impossible to determine.

While the sample is different, the methods used are usually the same as those used to process urine. The hair does go through an initial chemical processing that urine does not go through, to break down the sample into an analyzable form. The Immunoassay and GC/MS tests are two of the common methods also used to process hair samples, with the RIA test being the most popular hair analysis immunoassay method. This may be because it is somewhat more sensitive than the EMIT. The FPIA is also used for hair analysis because it also possesses more sensitivity. GC/MS and another mass spectrometry test called tandem mass spectrometry are used for confirmation, although TC/MS is less reliable than the GC/MS because of its sensitivity to the biases of hair testing.

Hair testing has run into some serious problems. One problem with hair testing for marijuana is that the metabolite does not show up in the same concentration for use as it does in other types of samples, such as blood and urine. Secondly, a person who has been exposed to secondhand smoke can test positive using hair as a sample, because the hair picks up the smoke in the room. In order for second-hand smoke to cause a positive result in urine or blood, the smoke still had to be inhaled and enter the bloodstream in order to show up on the test, requiring a much more highly concentrated exposure.

But one of the biggest strikes against hair testing is its potential bias for different types of hair. Studies have suggested that the coarseness and color of hair may bias hair tests. One possible explanation is the ability of melanin to bind with certain drugs to create a stronger bias, or a false result for a test. Melanin, the pigment that makes skin and hair dark, controls the amount of UV a person's skin or hair absorbs. Lighter hair has less melanin, and therefore less protection from ultraviolet (UV) light, which also degrades drug metabolites. Given these tentative findings, a person with dark, coarse hair could supposedly ingest an equivalent amount of a substance as a person with light, fine hair and the dark-haired person would test positive while the light haired person would test negative. Given scandals over racial profiling for traffic stops and drug busts, a potential racial bias in hair testing could be especially condemning. Even if this bias does not cut cleanly along racial lines, the fact that strong biases may exist for certain types of hair is a strong argument against the further use of hair testing. Given these problems with hair testing, you would think that it would be disallowed. Hair testing is not standing up as evidence in court, and is not being used by any federally mandated testing programs. Even though the Food and Drug Administration and the scientific community have criticized the serious shortcomings of hair testing, it is still available as a choice for private employers who choose to test for drugs, and is widely used as a method of testing, with a growing clientele.

4. Blood Tests

A drug test using a blood sample gauges current impairment much more accurately than a urine test because the sample gives a more direct measurement, showing the current concentration in the bloodstream. For the same reason that it gives more precise information about when the substance was consumed, blood tests only measure use for a few hours to a few days (for chronic cannabis smokers) after marijuana use, rather than up to a month or longer for urine tests. For this reason, blood tests tend to be used in situations where establishing a specific time for intoxication is necessary, such as following an automobile accident. Blood tests are typically not used for workplace testing. Some state laws prohibit the use of blood tests for workplace testing.

5. Tests in Development

Some other tests in development are perspiration and saliva tests.

a. Saliva Tests

Saliva, like blood, registers the presence of the drug itself rather than metabolites, and therefore offers information about a fairly short time period. Saliva can register positive for about 2–4 hours after smoking marijuana. Most drugs disappear altogether from saliva 12–24 hours after use. The development of saliva testing is ongoing, although it has begun to be implemented in alcohol testing in similar circumstances for which blood testing is used. Saliva testing is preferable because it is a less intrusive method of testing, which is considered a big advantage.

Using saliva as a sample is limited in scope because of its short detection time, and is likely to be used according to its advantages and disadvantages. Since the main advantage is detection of very recent use, while it is unable to detect use over time, it is unlikely to replace testing in situations where a company or institution is more interested in knowing about longer-term use. There are arguments that time of detection correlates to the time of certain drugs' effects on the body for saliva testing, but this is problematic. Still, it does detect use within a relatively small window of time, making it unlikely to replace testing via hair or urine samples. Saliva samples may become more common in situations where timeliness is key: detection of drug use in automobile drivers, accident victims or for employees prior to engaging in safety-sensitive activities.

Despite the potential advantages of saliva as a test sample, there are a few drawbacks that need to be overcome for its use to be acceptable. Contamination is a big risk for drug use that is oral, smoked, or inhaled through the nose. Contamination means that some of the substance may still be in the mouth, rather than ingested, causing the test to show more presence of the drug than the person actually ingested. Marijuana use is one example in which oral contamination is a danger.

b. Perspiration Tests

Perspiration tests require a person to wear a patch for several days. The patch is typically worn on the upper arm, lower midriff, or lower back for at least 24 hours and for as long as 7 days. This product has been approved by the Food and Drug Administration (FDA) to test for cocaine, amphetamines, and opiates, but has yet to receive FDA approval for the remaining two categories mandated for testing as part of the NIDA-5. It has not yet been cleared by the FDA to test for marijuana. Even though approval is pending, perspiration tests have been allowed in the correctional justice system since 1996, where it has been used for all five substances as a pilot of its accuracy. The ethics of this decision are questionable, since prisoners have been subject to serious consequences on failing a drug test that could be due to technical problems with the test itself.

Reports on the perspiration patch indicate that in some cases it caused rashes or other mild allergic reactions due to the adhesive used in the patch. Manufacturers and proponents of the test claim that the rate of allergic reactions among those tested is low.

Again, the drug testing programs of private companies are not subject to federal regulations and certifications. While many companies choose to go through the federally certified labs, a company may choose to use uncertified labs and testing procedures such as perspiration tests at their discretion.

D. PASSING AND FAILING

The only relatively sure way to pass a drug test is to have abstained from the use of any drugs for which you might be tested. But if you have ever used, how long is long enough to pass the test? Even with abstention, there is always the possibility of testing positive when you have not ingested anything that should produce a positive result. This is called a "false positive." False positives can happen as a result of inaccurate testing equipment, human error at any stage in the testing process, or the presence of a chemical in the test subject's urine that looks like one of the drugs being tested for.

Many people who submit to a test are hoping for or trying to create an error in the other direction, or a "false negative." This is when the person has used one of the substances for which they are being tested, but the results do not detect the substance, or detect it only at concentrations below the cutoff levels.

Of the drugs typically tested for, marijuana has the longest detection time after use, which can be up to 6 weeks when subjected to a urine test. There are too many variables to know how long marijuana metabolites will be detected for each person. Some factors that determine the detection time after marijuana use for any person are:

- the person's metabolism
- the frequency of marijuana use
- the length of time one has been a marijuana smoker
- the potency of the marijuana
- the individual's tolerance to marijuana
- the person's intake of fluids

A basic rule of thumb for detection times is that someone who uses infrequently and has a fast metabolism will have a shorter detection time. A person who uses frequently, has used over a long period of time, and has a slow metabolism will have a longer detection time. The detection time for marijuana use generally ranges from 3 days after use to 45 days after use. There is no exact calculation that will ensure you will test negative in a specific amount of time, but you can consider this range and the above factors and make your best determination. Be wary of specific results from any sure-fire calculation methods that do not take enough variables into account.

There are many products on the market that make claims about helping you pass a drug test. Drug testing products can be similar to dieting products. If the claims they make seem too good to be true, it is quite possible they are. Be a savvy shopper. Most of these products make guarantees, but are limited in their actual effectiveness.

There are three main methods marijuana users often turn to when trying to beat a drug test. These methods are: trying to flush metabolites from the body; adding something to the sample to interfere with the test or create a false negative; or substituting a clean sample for the actual sample.

1. Cleaning Out

Some products on the market claim to help clean the metabolites out of one's system. According to some experienced independent sources, some testing products really can yield results. These are the products that contain chelating agents, which can lower the metabolites present in a urine sample. They do so by introducing an agent that binds to the metabolites, making them basically too big for your kidneys to release them into your urine. While most products designed for this purpose will not specify their ingredients on the label, products such as Test Pure, Clear Choice, Purafyzit, Urine Luck, and Totally Clean contain chelating agents and may help temporarily lower the marijuana metabolites in urine. Depending on how often any individual uses and how much metabolite is normally present in his or her urine, these products may lower metabolites below the cutoff level if ingested anywhere from 12 hours to 4 days before testing occurs.

Home remedies, herbs, or health food supplements such as activated charcoal, vinegar, goldenseal, lecithin, niacin, and vitamin C may work as detoxifiers but have no proven influence on cleaning out drug metabolites as a result of short-term use. Some expensive herbal teas on the market claim to "clean the urine," but it is unclear whether they actually have any effect, or that any positive effect they do have is only a result of encouraging the user to drink a large volume of fluid, which can dilute the concentration to lower levels.

Barring the use of specially designed products, a common strategy known to lower levels somewhat is one of the simplest and most widely known: abstain from any substances that might make you test positive, and increase your fluid intake to dilute the concentration of drugs below the level of detection. This may be enough if the concentration levels are already fairly low. This method is less likely to work for chronic users who have smoked marijuana regularly over a long period of time, although along with abstaining, this method will still lower levels and can only help. It isn't necessary to overload on water for weeks before the test to benefit. Drinking plenty of water the day or two before the test is all that is necessary. You are diluting your sample by adding water, not necessarily eliminating metabolites faster. You can dilute for the entire week if you want—but it really only matters that you have ingested enough fluids to dilute your sample on test day.

Diuretics can increase your fluid output because they stimulate urination. Weak diuretics include such common fare as coffee and cranberry juice. Some health food products and nonprescription medications, such as those intended to relieve premenstrual water retention, are other diuretic options.

Some people think that exercising a lot will help "flush out the system" and give them a clean test. This is understandable logic, and if you have plenty of time before the test, this may be a worthy method, but if you only have a week or two, it probably won't have the results you were hoping to achieve. Eating less and exercising more just before a test can actually have the opposite result you want. These activities will speed your metabolism, and burn fat, which then releases more metabolites into your system for elimination. More metabolites end up in your urine, and your count will be higher as a result. Without discouraging these healthful lifestyle choices, eating heartily and laying off exercise on the day before and day of the test discourages the release of additional metabolites. For the same reasons, significant weight loss can increase the chance of testing positive.

If possible, avoid giving a sample from the first urination of the day. Metabolites tend to build up during sleep and this first release may contain higher levels of metabolites than at any other time. Another hint is to give your sample from mid-stream if you can. That is, start to pee in the toilet, halt the flow and give the sample, then finish peeing in the toilet, not giving your sample from the very beginning or very end of the stream.

While someone giving a genuine sample won't run into some of the problems that a person trying to adulterate or substitute a sample will, it is important that your sample show no evidence of tampering. Testing facilities are on the lookout for cheaters, but tests on pH and specific gravity, which can confirm tampering, are still only performed on a discretionary basis—that is, labs decide when to run these tests, but are not required to test all samples for these variables, and don't because it's not cost-effective to do so. Amendments to the current federal guidelines may mandate testing creatinine levels, pH, and specific gravity in order to lower the chances of samples passing that have been diluted or altered. Your state could also pass legislation requiring more stringent measures.

If you are using the above-described method, your only concern related to tampering is that your sample is not too dilute. Some people take a B-complex vitamin, which will give urine a rather bright yellow color. A 50–100 milligram dose of a B-complex vitamin should suffice. Taking vitamins is a regular part of many people's lifestyle so is not suspect, while it may prevent a sample from the suspicion of being too dilute. Other vitamins, such as vitamin C, do not have this effect. Testing procedures continue to adjust with attempts to beat the test, and it is possible that your sample will be singled out and checked, but if your test looks right, it is less likely to be subject to these processes.

If you are going to try to adjust your sample, this method is the least risky. Drinking fluids, making sure to urinate at least once before giving your sample, and using products with chelating agents if you did not have proper warning or suspect the concentration to be high in your urine because of very recent use, chronic long-term use, or recent weight loss can be effective. It is, of course, more effective if you have had longer to prepare for the test by abstaining. Cleaning out your system is probably the soundest approach if you are going to submit to a drug test.

2. Committing Adulteration or Substitution

An adulterant is an additive that is put in the sample to mask or interfere with the test results. Substances most commonly used as adulterants include ammonia, Visine®, baking soda, detergent, bleach, salt, and vitamin C but there is no evidence confirming that any of these substances work, and most of them could be detected fairly easily by sight or smell. Adulterants may cause the temperature to fall out of acceptable range, and temperature has become a pretty common measurement. An odd appearance or scent may precipitate optional tests on specific gravity, creatinine levels, or pH to be conducted on your sample. If any of these tests are run, tampering would be confirmed for any of the above substances.

Some adulterants can supposedly cause false negatives on the common EMIT test, but not reliably, and not on the more accurate GC/MS test. Theoretically, if you pass the EMIT, your sample should not be submitted to the confirmation GC/MS, but that only applies for companies that are following this standard. Using adulterants also comes with several disadvantages.

The risk of being caught in the process of adding something to your sample can be great. Many companies directly monitor the sample-giver in order to avoid tampering, and some companies have stricter policies for employees who tamper with a test than for those who have positive test results. Several companies that conduct drug tests claim to screen samples for adulterants, but these tests—for pH or specific gravity, for example—remain discretionary, and there is no data showing how well or how often they do so.

You are better off manipulating your sample before it leaves your body than afterward—that is, by drinking fluids, using products with chelating agents if necessary, and taking care about the sample you give.

If you have not prepared or been given forewarning about a test, it is possible to substitute a urine sample entirely, but not advisable. "Clean" urine samples are available on the market, but again, there is no absolute reliability about the product you are getting. Testing is often directly monitored to prevent sample alteration or substitution. Some facilities will make you strip and don a hospital gown before giving the sample, which could reveal any preparations you have made. The more you know about the test procedure beforehand, the better able you will be to assess if this is an option open to you.

Penalties for falsifying a test can be serious, and choosing to substitute is a risky choice. While pH and creatinine level testing should not be able to show that the urine is not yours (although it could reveal that the urine is not human), it may be difficult to maintain the proper temperature (between 91 and 97 degrees Fahrenheit). Some mail-order substitutes are set up to maintain the temperature of the substitute, and provide concealed methods of containment. If you arranged for the substitute sample yourself, you will need to keep this in mind. Only you can decide if the benefit of substitution is worth the risk, but even then, it should only be seen as a last-ditch alternative.

The states of Nebraska, Pennsylvania, South Carolina, and Texas have passed laws that criminalize the use of adulterating substances of any kind with the intent of falsifying a drug test. The laws include provisions prohibiting the sale of adulterants, including the sale of clean urine. Federal law has yet to pass such a prohibition even though most mandatory drug testing derives from federal legislation. Finally, there is the option of drug testing yourself. You can find a lab in your local Yellow Pages under "laboratories," and pay a moderate fee (about $40) for a confidential "pre-employment test" on yourself. If the test is analogous to the one your employer conducts, the time between tests is short, and you abstain in the interim, it should give an accurate prediction. Drug-testing facilities may offer confidential drug testing for a fee. Finally, home-testing kits are available, but the method and accuracy will most likely not equal those you are subjected to through a lab. Urine metabolite levels fluctuate day to day, and throughout the day, making home results less than 100 percent reliable as a prediction of lab results.

3. False Positives

There are very few substances that can create a false positive for marijuana. When the Thin Layer Chromatography test was more common, ibuprofen (Advil, Motrin, Nuprin) was said to interfere with marijuana detection. A variety of over-the-counter medicines can cause false positives for amphetamine and other illicit drugs on the EMIT test, but there are no known over the counter substances that cause false positives for marijuana, for either the EMIT or GC/MS test. Some sources indicate that high-dosage aspirin may reduce EMIT's sensitivity for detecting marijuana, but I did not find any data to support this claim.

Last August, ARUP Laboratories released results from a study, which concluded that the consumption of cold-pressed hemp seed oil, a product available in health food stores and groceries, can cause a false positive for cannabis metabolites. This product does not have any pharmacological effects, and is considered a healthful dietary supplement, derived from cannabis sativa's cousin. When used within the manufacturer's recommendation, (10 mL daily consumption), hemp seed oil continued to cause a false positive in the days after the test subject had quit eating it. Presumably, other health food snacks or products that contain hemp seeds or hemp seed oil as a prominent ingredient could produce similar results.

In a second trial, researchers concluded regular consumption of hemp seed capsules, available as a health supplement, resulted in a positive test for marijuana, but at much lower levels than cases where hempseed oil was consumed. Objections to tests based on the consumption of hemp oil has been upheld in two court martial cases, where marijuana charges were overturned after evidence that the test subject had consumed hemp oil was brought forth. There have already been attempts to limit the consumption of hemp-based products by military personnel in order to sidestep this problem.

Passive (second-hand) marijuana smoke will likely not excuse a positive test result. The lowest standard cutoff level of 50 ng/mL in screening tests is considered to be too high to register typical second-hand exposure. Supposedly, a test subject could only test at 50 ng/mL under extreme circumstances—very close quarters for a sustained time with very heavy smoke. Passive exposure has been known to register marijuana at a level of 25 ng/mL or lower.

Marinol®, the prescription medication that contains THC (also called Dronabinol), will undoubtedly create a positive result for marijuana. This is not technically a "false" positive, as Marinol® contains the same chemical component as marijuana. It is only a "false positive" insofar as the use of this marijuana-based medicine is not illicit, but is a legitimized treatment for some health conditions. Marinol® is currently the only prescription medication available that contains a derivative of marijuana, outside of the use of medical cannabis itself in locations where such use has been legalized. There are no other known prescription medications that create a positive test for marijuana in both the immunoassay and GC/MS tests.

E. RECOURSE

Although drug testing methods are far from infallible, it can be very difficult to challenge positive test results. "False positives," where an employee tests positive for marijuana use when they have not used marijuana, are improbable if the labs have shown proper care in handling the samples, but proper care cannot be taken for granted. In the overwhelming majority of cases, lab errors are human errors in transporting, recording, calibrating machinery, or performing analysis.

Persons who test as a pre-employment requirement, or private employees in states with no restrictions for private companies have very limited options for challenging results. There is more leverage for people who are already employees, and who work for the government or a company that is regulated.

One of the principle rules in drug testing is to never give it up. Saying, "I couldn't have tested positive from only that one joint I smoked," or "I haven't smoked in three months," implicates you. End of story. It doesn't matter if the data was flawed or an administrative error occurred. If you admit use, you have no recourse. Keep your lips sealed about use, focusing instead on the flaws of the results.

Some sources recommend that you request information about drug testing policy before being tested. It is good to be aware of the company's policy. This could be especially important at pre-employment. Pre-employment testers have little recourse to challenge results. Knowing a company's policy for testing and notification may make you reconsider applying for the position altogether. Knowledge about methods of testing, including what type of sample they take, whether or not they use an in-house or outside laboratory, whether or not the laboratory is certified, and what notification they provide after testing, could help in formulating a strategy and relieve some anxiety about the testing. While you may feel reluctant to ask these questions because you don't want to create suspicion, you are entitled to the answers if they require you to undergo testing.

Once you are an employee, your ability to challenge results is better than it was prior to employment, but again this depends on a few factors. The biggest factor is whether the company you work for is mandated by the government to conduct drug testing. If you work for the government or a company that is required to test, the rules are more specific and constitutional protections are in your corner. If the company for which you work is private, there may still be state laws that place limits on testing conditions.

Challenging drug tests in court can be an expensive course of action and the results have been mixed. Some courts have ruled that mandatory urine testing of government employees violates the Constitution. Several winning cases invoked the Fourth Amendment, arguing that testing was not based on individualized suspicion. Courts throughout the U.S. have ruled against random testing programs for groups of public employees ranging from prison guards to cops to teachers. In many of these cases, unions and the ACLU have played important roles in representing employees' rights. But in a few cases, random testing without suspicion was upheld. Rulings in two cases, involving U.S. Customs guards and railroad workers, respectively, upheld the definition of urine tests as "searches," but considered them reasonable within the Fourth Amendment, stating that the right to privacy was outweighed in these instances by the government's interest in maintaining a drug-free workplace.

If a legal challenge to test results is made, all records documenting test results and quality control procedures must be made available. Such a package should contain the following documents, according to a report by the Committee on Drug Use in the Workplace:

- Collection site information, including the external chain of custody, temperature, and collection site identification
- Courier receipts if a courier was used
- An internal chain of custody form, if used
- Confirmation of specimen identification
- Any checks for integrity

(pH, specific gravity or creatinine level checks, for example)
- Screening data, including controls, calibration, quality control information and certifying scientist signatures
- Accessioning chain of custody for confirmation test
- GC/MS data, including controls, calibration information, quality control information, and certifying scientist signatures
- The Validation Report of positive identification, including signatures, the number measurement (ng/mL), and the cutoff levels
- Specimen long-term storage

Federal constitutional protections only apply to government employees. Private employees have brought challenges to the courtroom over drug testing throughout the U.S., basing their charges on state constitutional or statutory laws rather than federal law. Some cases have been brought on the grounds of breach of contract, and occasionally a lawsuit is filed based on common law actions that allege intentional and specific injury. These cases have met with mixed results. While states continue to deliberate and pass laws that offer some protections to employees, many states have no such protections. Private sector workers who are unionized may have some determination in the company's drug testing policy. Still, the law has treated drug testing similarly to other personnel matters in the private sector: they have specified very little, allowing broad discretion for private employers and almost no protections for employees in the private sector.

Some states have extended protective legislation to restrict private sector drug testing, including California, Connecticut, Iowa, Maine, Minnesota, Montana, Rhode Island, and Vermont. Through this legislation, private sector employees have gained some protections from unfair workplace testing. These protections include requiring private businesses to maintain the same right to privacy required by the government in the Federal Constitution; bans on random or suspicionless drug-testing policies; or limitations of random testing to safety-sensitive positions only. In addition to limiting testing, several states have passed laws requiring private industry to use confirmation tests following a positive screen, certified personnel in specimen collection, and certified labs for sample analysis. You should check the policy in your location to see if any legislation has been passed or is pending in your state.

F. THE POLITICS OF DRUG TESTING

Individuals often feel infringed upon as a result of drug testing, even when they expect to pass the test. However, many people do not feel motivated to act if they don't feel that they are personally at risk to fail.

Those who worry about passing tend to concentrate on tricking the labs on their own test than on challenging drug testing at a larger level.

Everyone has good cause to object to drug testing as a policy, including those with no concerns about passing. Everyone has the right to privacy. Urinalysis can disclose information about a person's private life beyond illicit drug use, including the use of prescription medications used for health conditions, information that the employee has the right to hold as confidential. These tests can also reveal that an employee is pregnant. While the tests are not supposed to be used for these purposes, there is no guarantee that such information is not derived from provided samples.

EMPLOYEE RIGHTS

The right against unreasonable search and seizure

This right is guaranteed in the Fourth Amendment to the Constitution. It only protects citizens from search and seizure by agents of the government, not other private entities or individuals. The urine test has been found by the courts to qualify under the legal definition of a "search." The Fourth Amendment requires a "probable cause" to consider a search reasonable, under which suspicionless testing, such as any routine or random testing does not qualify. This is because "probable cause" is considered inapplicable for "administrative searches," which are searches conducted for a regulatory rather than a law enforcement purpose. A precedent was first set for this special rule by the 1967 Supreme Court finding in the case of Camera v. Municipal Court (387 U.S. 523, 1967), which addressed city housing inspections. Workplace drug tests have qualified as an administrative search, requiring the less rigorous, "rational cause" rather than "probable cause" for justification.

The right to due process

Challenges to drug tests based on a violation of due process have met with little success. Still, standards and procedures must be followed before people can be deprived of their freedoms. In challenging a drug test, the results of the test must meet acceptable standards of validity and accuracy that the court recognizes as such. Many courts have considered testing that was not backed by a confirmatory

Drug testing does not provide information about impairment on the job. Because drug tests measure metabolites, it is actually possible to smoke a joint directly before taking a piss test and pass, whereas someone who used in their free time over last weekend would test positive.

Consider it: what started as a test for the military and safety-sensitive positions in government, such as air-traffic controllers, has mushroomed into policing desk lackeys and burger flippers across the country. Ironically, the persons for whom the test was initially designed benefit from the most protections under the law. Ninety-seven percent of the 500 largest companies conduct drug testing. These companies are each spending in the tens of thousands, to discover an average of five

test as insufficient evidence to prove illicit drug use. Requesting all the information regarding the test including practices and procedures, calibration information, the blind positives used for standard-setting, the paperwork that confirms and validates your sample, scientist's verifying signatures, and confirmation results in ng/mL allows you a chance to find potential areas where acceptable standards of accuracy and validity were not upheld.

When federal and state laws don't protect you

Prospective employees are out of luck; there is no legal ground on which to challenge pre-employment drug screens and win. Workers employed in the private sector have extremely limited options. When there is no state law, the already employed should turn to local labor law and local ordinances for possible grounds to challenge unfair testing. Some jurisdictions, such as San Francisco and Berkeley, California forbid workplace drug testing outside of testing mandated by federal law. If the workplace is unionized, participate in voting on drug-testing-related initiatives. In non-union positions, employees should avoid agreeing to anything in writing, or signing any contracts that allow the company to arbitrarily test. Getting as much information about the workplace's policies before being tested is a good idea. You may have cause for legal action if you think you have been tested unfairly; you should seek a professional legal opinion.

🌿

drug users per 100 employees—three of whom smoked pot. Drug tests are incapable of pinpointing that a person is under the influence of drugs at the time they are tested, or at a time when they are on the job.

Recent studies by several independent sources, including Le Moyne College's Institute of Industrial Relations, and the National Research Council's Committee on Drug Use in the Workplace do not support the beneficial claims made for workplace drug testing. The National Research Council Committee's 1994 report, "Under the Influence? Drugs and the American Work Force," compiled original research which the ACLU has worked to publicize in a pamphlet entitled "Drug Testing: A Bad Investment." The committee of distinguished medical, legal, and business experts concluded that "the data ... do[es] not provide clear evidence of the deleterious effects of drugs other than alcohol on safety and other job-performance indicators." The 1998 report published by Edward Shepard and Thomas Clifton of LeMoyne College, "Drug Testing and Labor Productivity; Estimates Applying a Production Function Model," actually found a 20 percent drop in productivity—attributed not to drug use, but to the introduction of workplace drug testing—among the 63 companies the study included.

Performance testing is one possible alternative to drug testing that, if developed, could focus on the real issue at hand—the ability to perform a job—rather than misplacing these concerns in a Drug War witch-hunt for politically incorrect drugs. If well thought out, such testing has the ability to address the concern of most employers while also removing the intrusiveness of pinpointing causes.

Instead, the arena for drug testing keeps enlarging. The Drug and Alcohol Testing Industry Association (DATIA) have turned their sights to small business as a new market to exploit. According to DATIA statistics, only 3 percent of small businesses currently drug test. DATIA is lobbying government for legislation that gives tax credits to small businesses for adopting a drug-free workplace program.

In addition, DATIA continues to push for measures that institute drug testing in public schools. They support congressional measures that target schools as grounds for waging the Drug War, with strong support for drug testing as a component of maintaining drug-free schools.

In several states including Indiana and Massachusetts, mandatory drug testing in public schools has been overturned as unconstitutional. There is strong lobbying and support from the burgeoning drug testing industry to expand testing in the small business community by pushing for a bill that offers federal tax credits for those who are willing to make their coworkers pee for their jobs. Federal bills aimed at the public school system, such as HR 1735, the "Empowering Parents to Fight Drugs Act," and HR1642, the "Parental Consent Drug Testing and Counseling Act" are making their way through Congress. Both of these bills encourage random drug testing in the schools beginning as early as grade 7, allowing parents to remove their children from testing or request that their child be tested. In order to avoid the further encroachment of drug testing, opposition to such legislation needs to be voiced.

Controversy has always surrounded mandatory drug testing. The growth of voluntary drug testing in the private sector is a disturbing development. There is little opportunity for individual recourse to any positive results, regardless of whether they were incorrectly collected or analyzed. There is a need to support the passage of local ordinances or state laws that limit the free license private companies now have for such testing.

Most positive drug tests reveal marijuana use. This is in part because marijuana has a longer period of detection that other tested substances. It is also because marijuana is by far the most commonly used illicit drug in America. Almost all legitimate research on the topic shows that marijuana-using employees and non-marijuana-using employees are so alike in terms of productivity, absenteeism, health care, accident rates, and compensation claims as to be indistinguishable from one another. Given these facts, the façade of drug testing becomes another thin veneer for stepping on the toes of basic rights in the name of the War on Drugs.

Marijuana-Related Penalties: Federal & State-by-State

- The penalties listed only apply to first-offense convictions unless otherwise stated.

- The listing of a penalty, immediately followed by the letter "**M**" indicates a "**mandatory minimum**" prison sentence. This means that the judge must sentence an individual convicted of the said offense to a prison sentence of at least the duration of that listed. The offender is not eligible for parole and must serve the full term of the sentence.

- Any amount listed for "possession" generally implies that it is intended for personal consumption. Possession of large amounts of marijuana will, in most cases, lead to charges of "possession with intent to distribute" (same as "sale").

- Units of weight vary from state to state. For comparative purposes:
1 ounce (oz.)	=	28.5 grams (g)		
1 pound (lb.)	=	16 ounces	=	453.59 grams
1 kilogram (kg)	=	1,000 grams	=	2.2 pounds

- Many states have additional or enhanced penalties for certain offenses, such as sale within a specified distance of a school. These offenses and all applicable penalties have been noted, when possible. However, it should not be assumed that such penalties do not apply just because they have not been listed for a particular state.

- The following listings attempt to provide the range of the possible prison sentence; however, a multitude of factors are involved in determining sentence duration that may result in a sentence outside of this range.

- Except where otherwise indicated, the stated fine indicates the maximum possible fine for the offense.

These penalties are subject to change as the laws change, and should be corroborated with a regularly updated source, or with a legal professional.

FEDERAL PENALTIES

Possession
Any amount: 0–1 year; $10,000

Cultivation/delivery/sale
<100 kg: 0–20 years; $1,000,000
≥100 kg: 5–40 years; $2,000,000
≥1,000 kg (or 100 to 1,000 plants): 10 years–life; $10,000,000

Paraphernalia
Sale: 3 years; $250,000 or twice the pecuniary gain

Manufacture/distribution
≥100 plants or 100 kg: 5 **M**
≥1,000 plants or 1,000 kg: 10 **M**
Distribution within 1,000 ft. of school or playground, or within 100 ft. of youth center, public pool, video arcade (note that "school" includes public or private college or sale to a person under age of 21): Penalty doubles (1 year **M** unless ≤ 5 g)

Notes
Mailing marijuana or paraphernalia is a federal offense, even when the mail originates and arrives in the same state.

STATE-BY-STATE PENALTIES

ALABAMA

Possession
≤ 1 kg for personal consumption: 0–1 year; $2,000
≥ 1 kg under another charge: 1–10 years; $2,000

Cultivation/delivery/sale
> 2.2 lbs.: 3 years **M**, possible 10–99 years; $25,000
> 100 lbs.: 5 years **M**; $50,000
> 500 lbs.: 15 years **M**, $200,000
>1000 lbs.: life **M**
To minors: 2–20 years; $10,000
Within 3 miles of a school: 5 years *
Within 3 miles of a public housing project: 5 years *

Drug trafficking enterprise
1st offense: 25 years–life; $50,000–$1,000,000
2nd offense: life **M**

Paraphernalia
Possession: 0–1 year; $2,000

Notes
Driver's license suspension: 6 months.

ALASKA

Possession
< 8 oz.: 0–90 days; $1,000
≥8 oz.: 0–1 year; $5,000
≥ 1 lb.: 0–5 years; $50,000
≥ 25 plants: 0–5 years; $50,000
On a school bus: 0–5 years; $50,000
Within 500 feet of school or recreation center: 0–5 years; $50,000

Manufacture/delivery/possession with intent to manufacture or deliver
< 0.5 oz. for remuneration: 0–1 year; $5,000
≥0.5 oz.: 0–1 year; $5,000
≥ 1 oz.: 0–5 years; $50,000
Maintaining a structure or dwelling for manufacturing or delivery: 0–5 years; $50,000

Notes
Suspended imposition of sentence with 2–3 years of probation available for 1st offense if offense is a misdemeanor.

---

*These sentences run consecutive to other sentences and cannot be probated.

ARIZONA

Possession or use

≤ 2 lbs.: probation*; $750–$150,000.
Possible: drug "rehabilitation," community service, urine tests.

Possession for sale

< 2 lbs.: 1.5–3 years; $750–$150,000
≥ 2 lbs.: 2.5–7 years; $750–$150,000
>4 lbs.: 4 –10 years; $750–$150,000

Sale/delivery for sale/transport for sale

<2 lbs.: 2.5–7 years; $750–$150,000
≥2 lbs.: 4–10 years; $750–$150,000
Possession or sale in a "drug free zone," i.e., within 300 feet of a school, any public property within 1,000 feet of a school, or at a school bus stop or on any bus which transports pupils to school: 1 additional year of prison plus 2000–$150,000.

Production or cultivation

<2 lbs.: probation or 9 months–2 years; $750–$150,000
≥2 lbs.: 1.5–3 years; $750–$150,000
>4 lbs.: 2.5–7 years; $750–$150,000

Notes

The Drug Medicalization, Prevention and Control Act of 1996 (Proposition 200) became effective on July 21, 1997. The Act provides that a 1st or 2nd time marijuana offender may not be imprisoned for simple possession or use, regardless of amount of marijuana. However, a court may sentence the person to probation* with court supervised drug "rehabilitation," a fine of $750–$150,000, and/or community service. A person can be incarcerated if charged outside of the **"possession or use"** category.

Necessity defense: Section 13 - 417 of the Arizona Criminal and Traffic Law Manual, 1997–1998 edition, arguably allows a patient to tell a jury that s/he uses marijuana for medical purposes.

ARKANSAS

Possession

≤ 1 oz.: 0–1 year; $1,000

Cultivation/delivery/sale

> 1 oz.: 4–10 years; $25,000
≥ 10 lbs.: 5–20 years; $15,000–$50,000
≥ 100 lbs.: 6–30 years; $15,000–$100,000
To minor: 5–20 years; $15,000
Within 1000 feet of a school, public park, community or recreation center, skating rink, or video arcade: 5–20 years; $15,000

Notes

Driver's license suspension: 6 months.

CALIFORNIA

Possession

≤ 28.5 g: $100; no booking if you can show officer I.D. and promise to appear in court.
≤ 28.5 g on school grounds when school is open 1st offense: $250
≤ 28.5 g on school grounds when school is open 2nd offense: 10 days; $500
> 28.5 grams: 0–6 months; $500

Possession for sale

no specified amount: 16 months; 2–3 years probation.

Cultivation

For personal use only: stay of imposition of the conviction, drug education, charges dropped.
Not for personal use: 0–16 months; 2–3 years probation possible.

Notes

No plant number or weight breakdown. Selling, giving away, importing, or transporting into California: 2–4 years.

All marijuana offenses: probation available

Possession, cultivation, or transportation is legal upon a doctor's recommendation or approval.

---

*Probation: People placed on probation or early release generally must perform 24–360 hours of community service.

COLORADO

Possession

< 1 oz.: $100 plus surcharge

≥ 1 oz.: 0–2 years in county jail; $500–$5,000 plus surcharge

≥ 8 oz.: 1–4 years; $1,000–$100,000 plus surcharge

Generally, one prior conviction over 1 oz. doubles the penalties.

Cultivation/manufacture/delivery/sale

≤ 100 lbs.: 2–8 years in Department of Corrections; $2,000–$500,000 plus surcharge

> 100 lbs.: 24 years **M**; $5,000–$1,000,000

Two prior violations involving manufacture: 2 years **M**

Proof of sale: 1–16 years

Sale or giving marijuana to person aged 15 years or younger:

2–8 years; $2,000–$500,000 plus up to another $5,000

Paraphernalia

Sale/possession: $100 plus surcharge

Notes

Extraordinary mitigating or aggravating circumstances allow the court to sentence outside proscribed sentencing ranges.

CONNECTICUT

Possession

≤ 4 oz. 1st offense: 0–1 years; $1,000

≤ 4 oz. 2nd offense: 0–5 years; $3,000

≥ 4 oz. 1st offense: 0–5 years; $2,000

≥ 4 oz. 2nd offense: 0–10 years; $5,000

Within 1500 feet of a school: add 2 years **M** consecutive to other incarceration

Cultivation/delivery/sale

< 1 kg: 0–7 years; $25,000

≥ 1 kg: 5–20 years **M**; $2,000

Paraphernalia

Possession: 90 days; $500

Within 1500 feet of a school: additional 1 year **M** consecutive to other incarceration.

Notes

Professional licenses suspension.

Medical necessity, § 21a - 253, C.G.S. states a person may possess a quantity of marijuana less than or equal to that quantity prescribed by a physician who is licensed to supply marijuana for treating glaucoma or side effects of chemotherapy.

DELAWARE

Possession

Any amount: 0–6 months; $1,150

Cultivation

0–5 years; $10,000

Trafficking

≥ 5 lbs.: 3 years **M**; $25,000

≥ 100 lbs.: 5 years **M**; $50,000

≥ 500 lbs.: 15 years **M**; $100,000

Delivery

Any amount: 5 years; $10,000

To a minor: 0–5 years

To a minor if minor is under 16: 1 year **M**

To a minor if minor is under 14: 2 years **M**

Within 1,000 feet of school: 0–30 years; $250,000

Within 300 feet of park land, a park, or recreation area: 0–15 years; $250,000

Paraphernalia

Possession: 0–1 year; $2,300

Manufacture or delivery: 0–2 years

Delivery to a minor: 0–5 years

Notes

Maintaining a dwelling or vehicle in which marijuana smoking or other marijuana-related conduct occurs: 0–3 years; court's discretion on fine.

Suspended sentences possible except for trafficking.

DISTRICT OF COLUMBIA

Possession

Any amount: 0–180 days; $1,000

1st time possession offenders are eligible for probation followed by dismissal.

Cultivation/delivery/sale

Any amount: 0–1 year; $10,000

To minor: penalty doubles

Paraphernalia

Possession: 0–1 year; $500

Delivery to a minor: 0–8 years; $15,000

Notes

Driver's license suspension: 6 months.

FLORIDA

Possession

≤ 20 g: 0–1 year; $1,000

> 20 g: 0–5 years; $5,000

Sale

Any amount: 0–5 years; $5000

Delivery

≤ 20 g without remuneration: 0–1 year; $1,000

Paraphernalia

Possession: 0–1 year; $1,000

Sale to minor: 15 years; $10,000

Within 200 feet of school, public housing, or public park: 15 years; $10,000

Trafficking

50–2,000 lbs.: 0–30 years; $25,000

> 2,000 lbs.: 0–30 years; larger fine

10,000 lbs.: ≥ 15 years **M**; $200,000

Notes

Driver's license suspension: 6 months.

Professional licenses suspension.

A vehicle can be confiscated for any felony amount.

GEORGIA

Possession/sale

< 1 oz.: 0–1 years; $1,000

If arrested in a municipality you can choose to appear in city court instead of state court: maximum 60 days; $500

≥ 1 oz.: 1–10 years; $1,000

>5 lb.: 3 years **M**; $25,000

>100 lb.: 5 years **M**; $50,000

>500 lb.: 15 years **M**; $100,000

Paraphernalia

Possession: 0–1 years; $1,000

Third offense: 1–5 years; $5,000

Cultivation

0–10 years; $100,000

Trafficking

Includes the sale, manufacture, growth, delivery, import of marijuana into Georgia or any quantity of marijuana > 50 lbs:

> 50 lbs.– < 2,000 lbs.: 5 years **M** plus $100,000

≥ 2,000 lbs.– < 10,000 lbs.: 7 years **M** plus $250,000

≥ 10,000 lbs.: 15 years **M** plus $1,000,000

Use of a communications facility (i.e., telephone, radio, etc.) during drug felony may add 1–4 years; $30,000

Manufacture/distribute/dispense/possess with intent to distribute within 1,000 feet of an elementary or secondary school, a school board used for elementary or secondary education, property owned or leased by an elementary or secondary school, or any park, playground, recreational center, drug free commercial zone: 0–20 years; $20,000

Manufacture or distribution involving a minor: 5–20 years; $20,000

Notes

Driver's license suspension: at least 6 months; license reinstated only with "treatment."

Professional licenses suspension.

2nd drug felony is punishable by life in prison.

HAWAII

Possession

< 1 oz.: 0–30 days; $1,000

> 1 oz.: 0–1 year; $2,000

2.2. lbs.: 0–5 years; $10,000

40 lbs.: 0–10 years; $25,000

Cultivation

≤ 25 plants: 0–5 years; $10,000

≥100 plants: 0–10 years; $25,000

Sale

< 2 oz.: 1 year; $2,000

≥ 2 oz.: 5 years; $10,000

> 2.2 lbs.: 10 years; $25,000

Within 750 feet of a school or within 10 feet of a parked school vehicle 1st offense: 0–5 years

Within 750 feet of a school or within 10 feet of a parked school vehicle 2nd offense: 2–10 years

Notes

Any marijuana in a vehicle causes all passengers to be charged with possession unless the marijuana is found on the person of an occupant.

IDAHO

Using marijuana or being under the influence of marijuana in a public place: 0–6 months or $1,000

Possession

< 3 oz.: 0–1 year; $1,000

> 3 oz.: 0–5 years; $10,000

By a prisoner: 1–5 years; $1,000

By a minor (misdemeanor amounts): 30 days detention; $300

Paraphernalia

Possession: 0–1 year; $1,000

Cultivation/delivery/sale

< 1 lbs. or 0–24 plants: 0–5 years; $15,000

≥ 1 lbs. or 25–49 plants: 1 year **M**; $5,000

≥ 5 lbs. or 50–99 plants: 3 years **M**; $10,000

≥ 25 lbs. or ≥ 100 plants: 5 years **M**; $15,000

Possible maximum: 15 years; $50,000

Manufacture/sale of paraphernalia

9 years; $30,000

To minor: prison time doubles.

On school grounds: penalty doubles.

Notes

A person's presence in a place where he or she knows that illegal drug activity is taking place is punishable by 0–3 months; $300

Required evaluation with all drug convictions; court can order treatment.

ILLINOIS

Possession

< 2.5 grams: 0–30 days; $500

≥ 2.5 grams: 0–6 months; $500

≥ 10 grams: 0–1 year in county jail; $1,000

≥ 30 grams: 1–3 years in penitentiary or probation; $10,000

≥ 500 grams: 2–5 years or probation; $50,000

≥ 2,000 grams: 3–7 years or probation; $100,000

≥ 5,000 grams: 4–15 years or probation; $150,000

Cultivation

1–5 plants: 0–1 year; $1,000

5–20 plants: 1–3 years; $10,000

20–50 plants: 2–5 years; $10,000

50 plants: 3–7 years; $100,000

Manufacture/sale/delivery

< 2.5 grams: 0–6 months; $500

> 2.5 grams: 0–1 year; $1,000

> 10 grams: 1–3 years; $10,000

> 30 grams: 2–5 years; $50,000

500 grams – < 2,500 grams: 3–7 years; $100,000

Trafficking = bringing > 2,500 grams to manufacture/deliver: double penalty and fine.

To minor: double penalty and fine.

Within 1,000 feet of school, public park, or public housing or sale in a vehicle used for school purposes: 6–30 years no probation; $500,000

Calculated criminal conspiracy: 6–30 years no probation; $500,000; mandatory forfeiture.

INDIANA

Possession

≤ 30 grams: 0–1 year; $5,000; conditional discharge possible

> 30 g or 2nd possession of any amount: 6 months–3 years; $10,000

Paraphernalia

Possession: $500

"Reckless possession of paraphernalia": 0–1 years plus ≤ 1.5 years for aggravating circumstances or minus ≤ 1 year for mitigating circumstances; $5,000

Manufacture/sale: 0.5 years; $10,000

Cultivation/delivery/sale

≤ 30 grams: 0–1 year; $5,000

> 30 grams: 6 months–3 years; $10,000

≥ 10 lbs.: 2–8 years; $10,000

To minor: 0.5–3 years; $10,000
Within 1,000 feet of school, on a school bus, in a public park or a family housing complex: 2–8 years; $10,000

Notes
Driver's license suspension: 6 months–2 years (hardship license available)
Knowingly visiting a place where drugs are used: 0–180 days; $1,000

IOWA
Possession/sale
< 50 kg: 0–5 years; $1,000–$5,000 ≥ 50 kg: 0–10 years; $1,000–$50,000
≥ 100 kg: 0–25 years; $5,000–$100,000
1,000 kg: 0–50 years; $1,000,000
To minor within 1000 feet of school or public park: 10–25 years **M**

Notes
Driver's license suspension: 6 months.

KANSAS
Possession
Any amount of marijuana for personal use: 0–1 year; $2,500
2nd conviction: 10–42 months, which can double with aggravating factors; $100,000

Possession with intent to sell/ cultivation/sale
14–51 months which can double with aggravating factors; $300,000 Possession or attempt to buy or sell ≥ 100 plants or 100 lbs.:
21–27 months which can double with aggravating factors; $300,000 Possession with intent to sell or sale within 1,000 feet of a school:
46–83 months which can double with aggravating factors; $300,000

Any marijuana related conduct, which involves a minor or occurs in the presence of a minor may count as aggravating factor and increase the sentence.

For planting or growing more than 5 plants: 10–42 months, which can double with aggravating factors; $100,000

Paraphernalia
For personal use: 0–1 year; $2,500

KENTUCKY
Possession/sale
< 8 oz. 1st offense: 90 days–1 year; $500
< 8 oz. 2nd offense: 1–5 years
Possession with intent to sell (possession of ≥ 8 oz. is considered prima facie evidence of intent to sell)
≥ 8 oz. 1st offense: 1–5 years; $10,000
≥ 8 oz. 2nd offense: 5–10 years
≥ 5 lbs. 1st offense: 5–10 years; $10,000
≥ 5 lbs. 2nd offense: 10–20 years
To a minor 1st offense: 5–10 years
To a minor 2nd offense: 10–20 years
Within 1,000 feet of a school: 1–5 years; $3,000–$5,000

Trafficking
≤ 8 oz.: 1 year
< 5 lbs.: 1–5 years
≥ 5 lbs.: 5–10 years

Paraphernalia
1st offense: 90 days–1 year
2nd offense: 1–5 years

Cultivation
< 5 plants 1st offense: 90 days–1 year; $500
< 5 plants 2nd offense: 1–5 years; $3,00–$5,000
≥ 5 plants 1st offense: 1–5 years; $3,000–$5,000
≥ 5 plants 2nd offense: 5–10 years; $3,000–$5,000

Note
Defendants who are minors: driver's license suspension: 1–2 years.

Tax: Kentucky taxes marijuana plants and substance.

LOUISIANA
Possession (no quantity specified; usually under 2 oz. in one container)
1st offense: 0–6 months; $500
2nd offense: 0–5 years hard labor; $2,000
3rd offense: 0–20 years hard labor

Possession with intent to distribute/cultivation/sale

< 60 lbs.: 5–30 years hard labor; $50,000

≥ 60 lbs.: 10–60 years **M** hard labor; and $50,000–$100,000

≥ 2,000 lbs.: 20–80 years **M** hard labor; $100,000–$400,000

≥ 10,000 lbs.: 50–80 years **M** hard labor; $400,000–$1,000,000

To minor: doubled penalties

Felony possession or sale within 1,000 feet of school:

Driver's license suspension: 90 days–1 year

1st offense: maximum fine and a minimum of half of the maximum allowable term for offense served before pardon or parole.

Subsequent convictions: Maximum fine and maximum sentence without parole, probation, or suspended sentence.

MAINE

Possession

< 1.25 oz.: $400

> 1.25 oz. = evidence of intent to furnish marijuana. See penalties for sale.

Paraphernalia

Possession: 0–6 months; $200

Cultivation

100–500 plants: 1–5 years **M**; $5,000

≥ 500 plants: 2–10 years **M**; $20,000

Delivery/sale

< 1.25 oz.: 0–1 year; $1,000

≥ 1.25 oz.: 0–1 year; $2,000

≥ 2 lb.: 1–5 years **M**; $5,000

≥ 20 lb.: 2–10 years **M**; $20,000

To minor: 5 years; $5,000

Notes

Possible suspension of professional license.

Court can override minimums when sentencing first time defendants who present no danger to the public and who would suffer substantial injustice if sentenced to a **M**.

MARYLAND

Possession/use of any amount

0–1 year; $1,000

Paraphernalia

Possession: $500

Cultivation/delivery/sale

< 50 lbs.: 0–5 years; $15,000

≥ 50 lbs.: 5 years **M**

Smuggling into state (Trafficking)

≥ 100 lbs.: 0–25 years; $50,000

Using a minor: 0–20 years; $20,000

MASSACHUSETTS

Possession

Any amount 1st offense: probation.

Any amount subsequent offense: 0–6 months; $500. Probation possible.

Cultivation/delivery/sale

< 50 lbs.: 0–2 years; $5,000

≥ 50 lbs.: 2.5–15 years; $10,000; 1 year **M**

≥ 100 lbs.: 3–15 years **M**; $25,000

≥ 10,000 lbs.: 10–15 years; $200,000

To minor: 2.5–15 years; $1,000–$25,000

Within 1,000 feet of school: 2.5–15 years; $1,000–$10,000

Paraphernalia

Manufacture/sale: 1–2 years; $500–$5,000

Sale to minor: 3–5 years; $1,000–$5,000

Notes

License suspensions, any offense: at least 6 months.

Delivery or sale of any amount: driver's license suspension, 2 years.

Delivery or sale over 50 lbs.: driver's license suspension, 5 years.

MICHIGAN

Use

0–90 days; $100

Possession

Any amount: 0–1 year; $1,000 (probation available)

Cultivation/delivery/sale

Any amount: 0–4 years; $2,000

To minor: penalty doubles

Within 500 feet of school: penalty doubles

Paraphernalia

Manufacture/sale: 3 months; $5,000

Notes

License suspensions, any offense: 6 months.

*City of Ann Arbor is a decriminalized city ($50 civil fine).

MINNESOTA

Possession

≤ 42.5 grams: $200 and "drug education"

< 10 kg: 0–5 years; $10,000

≥ 10 kg: 0–20 years; $250,000

≥ 50 kg: 0–25 years; $500,000

> 100 kg: 0–30 years; $1,000,000

Possession of more than 1.4 grams in a motor vehicle is punishable by 0–1 year in prison and a $1,000 fine.

Sale/delivery

≥ 2 kg: 0–5 years; $10,000

≥ 5 kg: 0–20 years; $250,000

≥ 25 kg: 0–25 years; $500,000

50 kg: 0–30 years; $1,000,000

To minor: 0–20 years; $250,000

Within 300 feet or one city block of school, public park, or public housing: 15–30 years; $100,000–$1,000,000

Notes

Driver's license suspension: 30 days.

MISSISSIPPI

Possession

≤ 1 oz.: $100–$250

> 1 oz.: 0–1 year; $1,000

≥ 1 kg: 0–20 years; $1,000–$1,000,000

Additional penalties for possession in any part of a motor vehicle except the trunk.

Paraphernalia

Possession: 0–6 months; $500

Sale/delivery

< 1 oz.: 0–3 years; $3,000

≥ 1 oz.: 0–20 years; $30,000

≥ 1 kg: 0–30 years; $100,000–$1,000,000

> 10 lbs.: life without parole

To person under 21: penalty doubles

Within 1,500 feet of school: penalty doubles

Notes

Driver's license suspension: 6 months.

MISSOURI

Possession

≤ 35 grams: 0–1 year; $1,000

> 35 grams: 0–7 years; $5,000

> 30 kg: 5–15 years

100 kg: 10 years–life

Sale

< 5 grams: 0–7 years; $5,000

> 5 grams: 5–15 years

> 30 kg: 10 years–life

> 100 kg: life without parole

To minor: 5–15 years

Within 1,000 feet of school or public housing project: 10–30 years.

Additional penalties for sale near government-assisted or public housing.

Cultivation

Any amount: 5–15 years

Paraphernalia

Possession: 0–1 year; $1,000

Sale of: 0–5 years; $5,000

MONTANA

Possession

≤ 60 grams marijuana or < 1 gram hashish 1st offense: 0–6 months; $100–$500

≤ 60 grams marijuana or < 1 gram hashish subsequent convictions: 0–3 years; $1,000

>60 grams: 0–20 years; $50,000

Paraphernalia
Possession: 0–6 months; $500

Manufacture/cultivation/sale (intent to sell triggered at ≥ 1 kg)
≤ 1 lb.: 0–10 years and $50,000

> 1 lb. or > 30 plants: 2 years **M**–life and $50,000

Subsequent violations: up to two times the prison term plus $100,000 for the crime.

To minor: 4 years–life; $50,000

Within 1,000 feet of school: 3 years–life; $50,000

Notes
Continuing criminal enterprise: additional penalty equaling 2–3 times the length of punishment for the underlying offense.

NEBRASKA

Personal use
0–7 days; $500

Possession/sale
≤ 1 oz. 1st offense: citation for $100; "drug education" possible

≤ 1 oz. 2nd offense: $100–$500

≤ 1 oz. 3rd or subsequent offense: 0–7 days and $300

> 1 oz.: 0–7 days; $500

1 lb.: 0–5 years; $10,000

To minor increases penalty for offense to next highest classification.

Enhanced penalty for sale to minor within 1,000 feet of a school, college or playground, or within 100 feet of a youth center, public swimming pool or video arcade.

Paraphernalia
Possession: 0–6 months; $1,000

Sale to minor who is at least three years younger: 0–1 year; $1,000

Maintaining premises on which marijuana is stored or sold
0–3 months; $500.

NEVADA
* Effective July 1, 1999, probation will be no longer be guaranteed.

Possession/use
Any amount 1st offense: 1–4 years; $5,000

Any amount 2nd offense: 1–10 years

Any amount 3rd offense: 1–20 years

Cultivation/delivery/sale
< 100 lbs. 1st offense: 1–20 years

< 100 lbs. 2nd offense: 5–20 years; no parole or probation

< 100 lbs. 3rd offense: 15 years–life; no parole or probation

≥ 100 lbs.: 1–5 years; $10,000; no parole or probation

≥ 2,000 lbs.: 1–20 years; no parole or probation

≥ 10,000 lbs.: (a) life with parole eligibility after a minimum of 5 years, or (b) 15 years with parole eligibility after a minimum of 5 years; $200,000 under either scheme.

To minor 1st offense: 1–20 years

To minor 2nd offense: life

Within 1,000 feet of school, video arcade, public pool, youth center: penalty doubles.

Paraphernalia
Possession: 0–6 months; $1,000

NEW HAMPSHIRE
Possession
Any amount of marijuana or ≤ 5 grams hashish: 0–1 year; $1,000

5 grams hashish: $5,000

Cultivation/delivery/sale
< 1 oz. marijuana or < 5 grams hashish first offense: 0–3 years; $25,000

< 1 oz. marijuana or < 5 grams hashish subsequent offenses: 0–6 years; $50,000

≥ 1 oz. marijuana or ≥ 5 grams hashish first offense: 0–7 years; $100,000

≥ 1 oz. marijuana or ≥ 5 grams hashish subsequent offenses: 0–15 years; $200,000

≥ 5 lbs. marijuana or ≥ 1 lbs. hashish first offense: 0–20 years; $300,000

≥ 5 lbs. marijuana or ≥ 1 lbs. hashish subsequent
offenses: 0–40 years; $500,000

Within 1,000 feet of school: up to double the penalty.

Paraphernalia

Sale of: 0–1 year; $1,000

Notes

Enterprise Leader: 25 years **M**–life and $500,000 or five
times the street value, whichever is greater.

License suspension.

Possession with intent to sell: driver's license may be
revoked for any time period including life, at court's
discretion.

Minors aged 15–17 convicted of possession with intent
to sell will have their license revoked for 1–5 years.

Minors aged 15–17 convicted of possession, sale, or
use may have their driver's license revoked or license
application denied 60 days–2 years.

NEW JERSEY

Possession/use/under the influence

< 50 grams: 0–6 months; $1,000

50 grams: 0–18 months; $15,000

Within 1,000 feet of a school: if no jail time, then not
less than 100 hours of community service.

Manufacture/distribution/possession with intent to distribute

< 1 oz.: 0–18 months; $7,500

> 1 oz.: 0–5 years; $15,000

5 lbs.: 5–10 years **M**; $100,000

Sale

To minor or pregnant female: penalty may double.

Within 1,000 feet of school, < 1 oz.: 1–5 years **M**

Within 1,000 feet of school, ≥ 1 oz.: 3 years **M**

Notes

Driver's license suspension: 6 months–2 years.

NEW MEXICO

Possession

≤ 1 oz. 1st offense: 0–15 days and $50–$100

≤ 1 oz. subsequent offenses: 0–1 year; $100–$1,000

> 1 oz.: 0–1 year; $100–$1,000

≥ 8 oz.: 0–18 months; $5,000

Distribution/cultivation

Small amounts, no remuneration: same as possession

≤ 100 lbs. 1st offense: 18 months; $5,000

≤ 100 lbs. subsequent offenses: 3 years; $5,000

100 lbs. 1st offense: 3 years; $5,000.

100 lbs. subsequent offenses: 9 years; $10,000

Distribution to a minor 1st offense: 3 years; $5,000

Distribution to a minor subsequent offenses: 9 years;
$10,000

Within 1,000 feet of a drug free school zone: 18 years
and $15,000

Paraphernalia

Possession: 0–1 year; $50–$100

Delivery: 0–1year; $1,000

Any person over 18 who delivers paraphernalia to a
minor who is at least three years younger:
18 months; $5,000

All first-time offenders eligible for probation, no fine, and
expunged conviction.

NEW YORK

Possession

≤ 25 grams 1st offense: non-criminal violation; $100

≤ 25 grams 2nd offense: $200

≤ 25 grams subsequent offenses: $250; 0–15 days

> 25 grams or any amount possessed in public and the
marijuana is burning or open to public view:
0–3 months; $500

> 2 oz.: 0–1 year; $1,000

> 8 oz.: 0–4 years; $5,000

> 1 lb.: 0–7 years; $5,000

10 lbs.: 0–15 years; $5,000

Delivery/cultivation

≤ 2 grams for no consideration: 0–3 months; $500

< 25 grams: 0–1 year; $1,000

≥ 25 grams: 0–4 years; $5,000

> 4 oz.: 0–7 years; $5,000

1 lb.: 0–15 years; $5,000

To minor: 0–7 years; $5,000

Notes
Driver's license suspension: 6 months.

NORTH CAROLINA

Possession
< 0.5 oz.: 0–30 days, suspended sentence possible
> 0.5 oz. or 1/20 oz. of hashish: 1–120 days or community service or probation
> 1.5 oz. or 3/20 oz. hashish: 8–13 months
10 lbs. = trafficking

Trafficking
< 5 grams for no remuneration: suspended sentence possible
> 10 lbs.: 25–30 months **M** and at least $5,000
≥ 50 lbs.: 35–42 months **M** and at least $25,000
≥ 2,000 lbs.: 70–84 months **M** and at least $50,000
≥ 10,000 lbs.: 175–219 months **M** and least $200,000

Manufacture/cultivation/sale
4–10 months, may be suspended
Enhanced sentences for:
School zone: Anyone over 21 who sells or possesses with intent to sell within 300 feet of school property receives an enhanced sentence.
Pregnant women and minors: Sale or delivery by someone over 18 to a minor under 16 or to a pregnant female receives an enhanced sentence.

Paraphernalia
Possession/sale: 1–120 days

NORTH DAKOTA

Possession/sale/delivery/cultivation
< 0.5 oz.: 0–30 days; $1,000
0.5 oz.: 0–8 months; $2,000
1.5 oz.: 0–1 year; $5,000
≥ 100 lbs. 1st offense: 8 months **M**
≥ 100 lbs. 2nd offense: 3 years **M**
≥ 100 lbs. subsequent offenses: 10 years **M**
Possession of < 0.5 oz. while operating a motor vehicle: 1 year; $1,000
Anyone over 21 who uses a minor under 18 to produce or distribute any amount:

1st offense: 4 years **M**
Subsequent offenses: 5 years **M**

Paraphernalia
Possession: 0–1 year; $2,000
Sale of to minor by someone over 18 who is at least three years older : 0–5 years; $5,000
Sale within 1,000 feet of school: 4 years; $1,000

Notes
First offenders only: Possession of ≤ 1 oz.: Record of a guilty plea or verdict may be expunged after two years if no further drug or criminal offenses.
Atypically, North Dakota allows its judges to defer or suspend part or all of a penalty for a 1st offense, even if the penalty is listed as a **M**.

OHIO

Possession
< 100 grams: $100
≥ 100 grams: $250
≥ 200 grams: 6 months–1 year
> 1,000 grams: 1–5 years
> 5,000 grams: Presumption of prison
>20,000 grams: 8 years **M**
"Corrupting another with drugs": 6–18 months

Sale/cultivation
< 200 grams 1st offense: 6–12 months
< 200 grams subsequent offenses: 6–18 months
≤ 1,000 grams 1st offense: 6–18 months
≤ 1,000 grams 2nd offense: 1–5 years
5,000 grams–20,000 grams: Presumption of prison
> 20,000 grams: 8 years **M**, 2nd offense: 10 years **M**
To minor: 1 year; $1,000
Within 1,000 feet of school: 10 years **M**

Paraphernalia
Possession: 0–30 days; $250
Sale to minor: 6 months; $1,000

Notes
Driver's license suspension: 6 months–5 years.
Professional licenses suspension.

OKLAHOMA

Possession
Any amount 1st offense: 0–1 year; $500
Any amount 2nd offense: 2–10 years; $5,000

Cultivation
Any amount: 2 years–life; $20,000

Paraphernalia
Possession: 1 year; $1,000

Sale/delivery
< 25 lb.: 4 years–life; $20,000
≥ 25 lbs.: 5 years–life; $25,000–$100,000
≥ 1,000 lbs.: 5 years–life; $100,000–$500,000
To minor: penalty doubles
Within 1,000 feet of school: penalty doubles

Notes
Driver's license suspension.

OREGON

Possession
< 1 oz.: $500–$1,000
> 1 oz.: 0–10 years; $200,000

Manufacture
0–20 years

Paraphernalia
Possession: 0–1 year; $5,000 criminal fine plus civil fine
of $2,000–$5,000

Delivery
< 5 grams: $500–$1,000
> 5 grams: 0–1 year; $5,000
> 1 oz.: 0–10 years; $200,000

Sale
Any amount: 0–10 years; $200,000
To minor: 0–20 years; $300,000
Within 1,000 feet of school: 0–20 years; $300,000

PENNSYLVANIA

Possession
≤ 30 grams: 0–30 days; $500
> 30 grams: 0–1 year; $5,000

Cultivation/delivery/sale
Any amount: 0–15 years; $250,000
≥ 2 lbs. or ≥ 10 live plants: 1 year **M**; $5,000
≥ 10 lbs. or ≥ 21 live plants: 3 years **M**; $15,000
≥ 50 lbs. or ≥ 51 live plants: 5 years **M**; $50,000

Sale
To minor: penalty doubles
Within 1,000 feet of school or college: 1–2 years **M**

Paraphernalia
Possession: 0–1 year; $5,000
Sale to minor: 2 years; $5,000

Notes
Possible driver's license suspension: 6 months.

RHODE ISLAND

Possession
< 1 kg: 0–1 year; $200–$500
≥ 1 kg − ≤ 5 kg: 10–50 years **M** and up to $500,000
> 5 kg: 20 years–life **M** and ≤ $1,000,000

Manufacture/possession with intent to deliver
0–30 years; $3,000–$100,000
To minor: 1–5 years; ≤ $10,000
Within 1,000 feet of school: up to twice the listed penalty,
but not to exceed life

Notes
Driving while in possession of controlled substance 1st
offense: Driver's license suspension, 6 months.
Driving while in possession of controlled substance subsequent offenses: 1 year suspension

SOUTH CAROLINA

Possession
≤ 1 oz. marijuana or ≤ 10 grams hashish 1st offense:
0–30 days and $100–$200
≤ 1 oz. marijuana or ≤ 10 grams hashish subsequent
offense: 0–1 years; $200–$1,000

Paraphernalia
Possession/sale: $500 civil fine

Cultivation

≥ 100 plants: 25 years **M**–life; $25,000
> 1,000 plants: 25 years **M**–life; $50,000
> 10,000 plants: 25–30 years **M**; $200,000

Sale/delivery

≥ 10 lbs. brings presumption of trafficking
> 10 lbs. but < 100 lbs. 1st offense: 1–10 years **M**; $10,000
> 10 lbs. but < 100 lbs. 2nd offense: 5–20 years **M**; $15,000
> 10 lbs. but < 100 lbs. subsequent offenses: 25 years **M**; $25,000
≥ 100 lbs.: 25 years **M**; $25,000
≥ 2,000 lbs.: 25 years **M**; $50,000
≥ 10,000 lbs.: 25–30 years **M**; $200,000
To a minor: 0–10 years; $10,000
Within 1/2 mile radius of a school: 0–10 years; $10,000

Notes

Driver's license suspension: 6 months for marijuana and hashish convictions.

SOUTH DAKOTA

Possession

≤ 1 oz.: 0–30 days; $100 (misdemeanor)
< 8 oz.: 0–1; $1,000 (misdemeanor)
< 1 lb.: 0–2; $2,000 (felony)
≤ 10 lbs.: 0–5 years; $5,000 (felony)
> 10 lbs.: 0–10 years; $10,000 (felony)
1st felony: minimum 30 days imprisonment
2nd felony: 1 year **M**
Additional civil penalty of $10,000 for any possession offense. This is in addition to any criminal penalty imposed.

Cultivation/delivery/sale

Transferring < 8 oz. without remuneration: 0–30 days (misdemeanor)
≤ 1 oz.: 15 days–1 year; $1,000 (misdemeanor)
< 8 oz.: 30 days–2 years; $2,000 (felony)
< 1 lb.: 30 days–5 years; $5,000 (felony)
≥ 1 lb.: 30 days–10 years; $10,000 (felony)
To minor: 5 years **M**; $5,000

Within 500 feet of a school, youth center, public pool, video arcade: 5 years **M**.

Paraphernalia

Possession/use: 30 days; $100

Note

Driver's license suspension: 90 days

TENNESSEE

Possession

≤ 0.5 oz. 1st offense: 0–1 year; $250 minimum
≤ 0.5 oz. 2nd offense: $500 minimum
≤ 0.5 oz. subsequent offense: $750 minimum

Cultivation/delivery/sale

≤ 0.5 oz.: 0–1 year; $250 minimum
> 0.5 oz. or < 2 lbs. hashish: 1–5 years; $5,000
≥ 10 lbs. or ≤ 15 lbs. hashish: 4–10 years; $10,000
≥ 70 lbs. or > 15 lbs. hashish: 8–12 years and $200,000
≥ 700 lbs. or > 150 lbs. hashish: $500,000
To minor under age 18: penalty classification moves one level higher

Paraphernalia

Possession: 0–1 year; $2,500
Sale of: 1–6 years; $3,000

Note

Three prior felony drug convictions may place classify defendant as a **"habitual drug offender."** A habitual drug offender may be sentenced to the next higher punishment range and may be fined up to an additional $200,000.

TEXAS

Possession

≤ 2 oz.: 0–180 days; $2,000
> 2 oz.: 0–1 year; $4,000
> 4 oz.: 180 days–2 years; $10,000
> 5 lbs.: 2–10 years; $10,000
> 50 lbs.: 2–20 years; $10,000
> 2,000 lbs.: 5–99 years; $50,000

Sale/delivery

< 0.25 oz. for no remuneration: 0–180 days; $1,500
< 0.25 oz. for remuneration: 0–1 year; $3,000

≥ 0.25 oz.: 180 days–2 years; $10,000

≥ 5 lbs.: 2–20 years; $10,000

≥ 50 lbs.: 5–99 years; $10,000

≥ 2,000 lbs.: 10–99 years; $100,000

To minor: 2–20 years; $10,000

Within 1,000 feet of school or 300 feet of youth center, public pool, video arcade: penalty doubles

Money Laundering

Spending funds derived from the sale of more than 50 lbs. is in itself an offense punishable by 5 years–life or 99 years and a fine of $50,000–$1,000,000.

Paraphernalia

Possession: $500

Sale of: 0–1 year; $3,000

Notes

Driver's license suspension: 6 months.

UTAH

Possession

< 1 oz.: 0–6 months; $1,000

≥ 1 oz.: 0–1 year; $2,500

≥ 16 oz.: 0–5 years; $5,000

> 100 lbs.: 1–15 years; $10,000

Sale

0–5 years; $10,000

Within 1,000 feet of school, public park, amusement park, recreation center, church, synagogue, shopping mall, sports facility, theater, or public parking lot increases level of offense by one degree. Possession or sale with minor present: 5 years **M**

Paraphernalia

Possession: 6 months; $1,000

Sale of: 1 year; $2,500

Sale to minor: 0–5 years; $5,000

VERMONT

Possession

< 2 oz.: 0–6 months; $500

≥ 2 oz.: 0–3 months; $10,000

≥ 1 lb.: 0–5 years; $100,000

≥ 10 lbs.: 0–15 years; $500,000

Cultivation

> 3 plants: 0–3 years; $10,000

> 10 plants: 0–5 years; $100,000

> 25 plants: 0–15 years; $500,000

Delivery/sale

≥ 0.5 oz.: 0–5 years; $100,000

≥ 1 lb.: 0–15 years; $500,000

To minors: Anyone over 18 who sells to a minor who is at least three years younger: 0–5 years; $25,000

Potential additional penalty of up to 10 years for anyone (regardless of age) selling to a minor.

On a school bus also holds an additional penalty of 0–10 years.

Second conviction: doubled penalties are possible.

VIRGINIA

Possession

≤ 5 lb. 1st offense: 0–30 days; $500

≤ 5 lb. 2nd offense: 0–1 year; $2,500

≥ 5 lbs.: 1–10 years; $1,000

Cultivation

Any amount: 5 – 30 years; $10,000

Delivery/sale

≤ 0.5 oz.: 0–1 year; $2,500

> 0.5 oz.: 1–10 years; $2,500

≥ 5 lbs.: 5–40 years; $500,000

To minor: 10–50 years (1 year **M**); $100,000

Within 1,000 feet of school: 1–5 years **M**; $2,500–$100,000

Paraphernalia

Sale of: 1 year; $2,500

Sale to minor: 1–5 years; $2,500

Notes

Driver's license suspension: 6 months.

WASHINGTON

Possession

< 40 grams: 1–90 days; $1,000

≥ 40 grams: 0–5 years; $10,000

Cultivation/delivery/sale
Any amount: 0–5 years; $10,000
To minor: penalty doubles
Within 1,000 feet of a school adds 0–2 years
If armed with a deadly weapon: additional 0–2 years

Conspiracy to cultivate/deliver/sell
0–12 months

Paraphernalia
Possession: 0–90 days; $1,000

Notes
Driver's license suspension: 90 days for people under 21 years old.

WEST VIRGINIA

Possession
< 15 grams: automatic conditional discharge; $1,000
> 15 grams: 1–5 years; $15,000
First-time possession offenders may receive probation without further penalties.

Cultivation/delivery/sale
Any amount: 1–15 years; $25,000
To minor: 2 years **M**
Within 1,000 feet of school: 2 years **M**

WISCONSIN

Possession
Any amount 1st offense: 0–6 months; $1,000
Any amount 2nd offense: doubles penalty
Near a school, public park, public pool, youth center, community center, or school bus: ≥ 100 hours of community service is mandatory

Cultivation
≤ 10 plants: 0–3 years; $500–$25,000

≥ 11 plants: 3 months–5 years; $1,000–$5000
> 50 plants: 1–10 years; $1,000–$100,000

Delivery/sale
≤ 500 grams: 0–3 years; $500–$25,000
> 500 grams: 3 months–5 years; $1000–$50,000
≥ 2,500 grams: 1–10 years; $1000–$100,000
To prisoner: penalty doubles
To minor if seller is ≥ 3 years older: penalty doubles
Within 1,000 feet of school, public park, public pool, youth center, community center, school bus: 1 year **M**

Paraphernalia
Possession: 0–30 days; $500
Delivery or possession with intent to distribute: 0–9 months; $10,000
Sale to minor if seller is ≥ 3 years older: 0–90 days; $1,000

Notes
Courts have discretion to reduce a sentence if reduction is in the community's best interest and the public won't be harmed.
Mandatory doubling of sentences for 2nd and subsequent offenses.
Driver's license suspension: 6 months–5 years.

WYOMING

Personal use
≤ 3 oz.: 0–12 months; $100

Possession
Any amount: 0–6 months; $750

Cultivation
Any amount: 0–6 months; $1,000

Sale/delivery
Any amount: 0–10 years; $10,000
To minor: penalty doubles
Within 500 feet of school: 2 years **M**

Federal Law

A. Bill of Rights   **160**

B. Here Come the Feds   **161**

C. Sentencing Guideline Commission   **162**

D. Sentencing Guideline Levels   **163**
1. *Basic Levels for Marijuana and Hash*   *164*
2. *Enhancements*   *165*

E. Statutes and Guidelines   **165**
1. *Guidelines*   *165*
2. *Laws*   *166*

F. The Safety Valve   **170**

G. Time Off   **170**

A. BILL OF RIGHTS

The provisions of the English Magna Carta were written into the Bill of Rights, which comprises the first ten amendments to the United States Constitution. They are as follows:

Amendment I. Congress shall make no law respecting an establishment of religion, or prohibiting the free exercise thereof; or abridging the freedom of speech, or of the press; or the right of the people to peaceably assemble, and to petition the Government for a redress of grievances.

Amendment II. A well regulated Militia, being necessary to the security of a free State, the right of the people to keep and bear Arms, shall not be infringed.

Amendment III. No Soldier shall, in time of peace, be quartered in any house, without the consent of the Owner, nor in time of war, but in a manner to be prescribed by law.

Amendment IV. The right of the people to be secure in their persons, houses, papers, and effects, against unreasonable searches and seizures, shall not be violated, and no Warrants shall issue, but upon probable cause, supported by Oath or affirmation, and particularly describing the place to be searched, and the persons or things to be seized.

Amendment V. No person shall be held to answer for a capital, or otherwise infamous crime, unless on a presentment or indictment of a Grand Jury, except in cases arising in the land or naval forces, or in the Militia, when in actual service in time of War or public danger; nor shall any person be subject for the same offense to be twice put in jeopardy of life or limb; nor shall be compelled in any criminal case to be a witness against himself, nor be deprived of life, liberty, or property without due process of law; nor shall private property be taken for public use, without just compensation.

Amendment VI. In all criminal prosecutions, the accused shall enjoy the right to a speedy and public trial, by an impartial jury of the State and district wherein the crime shall have been committed, which district shall have been previously ascertained by law, and to be informed of the nature and cause of the accusation; to be confronted with the witnesses against him; to have compulsory process for obtaining witnesses in his favor, and to have the Assistance of Counsel for his defense.

Amendment VII. In Suits at common law, where the value in controversy shall exceed twenty dollars, the right of trial by jury shall be preserved, and no fact tried by jury, shall otherwise be reexamined in any Court in the United States, than according to the rules of common law.

Amendment VIII. Excessive bail shall not be required, nor excessive fines imposed, nor cruel and unusual punishments inflicted.

Amendment IX. The enumeration in the Constitution, of certain rights, shall not be construed to deny or disparage others retained by the people.

Amendment X. The powers not delegated to the United States by the Constitution, nor prohibited by it to the States, are reserved to the States respectively, or to the people.

As a result of the experiences of the Civil War, and the realization that all citizens had certain rights, the Fourteenth Amendment was ratified in 1868. Since the early twentieth century it has been considered by Constitutional scholars to be a part of the Bill of Rights. The first section reads, "All persons born or naturalized in the United States and subject to the jurisdiction thereof are citizens of the United States and the state in which they reside. No State shall make or enforce any law which shall abridge the privileges or immunities of citizens of the United States; nor shall any State deprive any person of life, liberty or property, without due process of law; nor deny to any person within its jurisdiction the equal protection of laws."

B. HERE COME THE FEDS

Each state has its own rules and laws regarding the amount of marijuana you can possess or grow and still not be a major criminal. Marijuana is illegal everywhere. Familiarizing yourself with how bad it could be will help you make an informed decision as to how bad you want to be. The most pathetic case is the defendant who says, "I didn't think it was so bad to possess/grow that much."

The federal law applies to everyone, all the time, in every state. There are supposed to be rules, criteria, and guidelines that federal prosecutors follow in deciding whether or not to prosecute your case. The truth is that the Feds prosecute you if they want to. No reason is required. Growing or possessing on federal land is usually prosecuted in federal court. Cases are passed off to the state only if the operation is small and the prosecutors have a busy schedule. Federal border busts in San Diego, California can be resolved as a misdemeanor on the right day, in the right court, with the right defendant and good legal moves.

Cultivation projects on BLM (Bureau of Land Management) land usually wind up in federal court unless they are very small. The federal 100-plant-minimum mandatory sentencing seems to influence the cops.

Growing or distribution efforts that seem to be interstate or international in scope are often seen by the Feds as fair game. Shipping some bud back East may be a righteous thing to do, but the Feds will be alerted if the U.S. Postal Service, UPS, or Federal Express gets suspicious and busts the load. They are also likely to prosecute if the bust occurred at a federal or state border, if the suspects were obviously out-of-town talent, or even if the stay-at-home, purely local crime is just "too big" for the local courts to adequately punish.

The last and most disgusting use of federal (versus state) prosecutorial power is when the search warrant is illegal under state law and the evidence is, or probably would be, suppressed by the state court. Since state courts follow state rules and precedents, and federal courts look to federal law and precedents, it's quite possible that your state gives you (or would if it could) more protection from a cop's illegal actions than do the Feds. The Feds, remember, allow the "good faith" acceptance of a bad warrant, which has all but nullified the protections of the Fourth Amendment.

The law allows state and federal prosecutors to decide who to prosecute, and for what. Even if the state prosecutes and you're found not guilty, you can still be prosecuted by the Feds. Federal rules apply to state busts and state cops when these come to federal court.

If you've been prosecuted by the state court and a jury has brought in a verdict of not guilty, it may be more difficult for you to be prosecuted in federal court for the same crime, but it's not impossible.

The Feds also have a series of creative "crimes" they can charge you with. Conspiracy is considered a separate crime. There is always some inventive prosecutor who can think up a (slightly) different crime to hit you with. You'd think that if you were not guilty of hitting someone, you wouldn't be guilty of violating their civil rights by hitting them. Courts have ruled otherwise.

C. SENTENCING GUIDELINE COMMISSION

The U.S. Sentencing Commission was set up to devise uniform sentencing guidelines. The purpose was to give the courts less discretion in handing out sentences. The Commission has been a prosecutor's dream. Regular Joes are regularly slapped with 5- to 10-year sentences as their property is confiscated and their dependents thrown out on the street.

In 1989, the Commission announced guidelines for implementing the laws of the Omnibus Crime Control Act. These guidelines determine the sentences for various crimes. In marijuana cases, the sentencing level is determined by the quantity of marijuana seized by the government.

D. SENTENCING GUIDELINE LEVELS

Though few people would seriously object to a long sentence for a violent repeat offender, long mandatory sentences for marijuana crimes seem cruel and unusual. There are over 500,000 people in state and federal jails for pot crimes. The Feds won't release the figures because they know the public would react adversely if the truth were known.

If you're busted or prosecuted by the Feds, your relevant offense conduct (defined below) and your offense level, which is calculated from it, are extremely important. "Relevant offense conduct" refers to anything that you've done that has relation to what you're charged with. The judge decides on the relevant offense conduct and, thereby, on the offense level. These are terms used for the purpose of defining, for sentencing purposes, how serious your criminal activities were. The crime you were charged with or were convicted of does not matter. The jury and prosecutor are not the final deciders of the amount of product you must stand trial for.

Once you have been convicted and a date has been set for sentencing, the judge will order you to report to the probation office for an interview with a probation officer. If you are held in custody until sentencing, then s/he will visit you. The probation officer investigates you by reading the police reports and talking to the cops and the prosecutor. You get an hour or less to tell your side of the story. The probation officer creates a Pre-sentence Investigation Report, which is presented to the court. If you disagree with the opinions voiced in the report, you can try to show the judge at sentencing that the numbers in the report are bogus. For instance, an independent report can be prepared by a specialist hired by you. The judge decides the relevant offense conduct, and thereby the offense level. S/he then goes to the charts, and the drug quantity table shows where you fit into the great scheme of crimes and criminals in America.

You can be given additional time for many individual factors that are or are not present. Accepting responsibility for your crime is good; having a leadership role is bad—that sort of thing.

Your mouth can send you away for a long time, as can your coconspirators. The rules are simple because they are so uniformly, unflinchingly hard: If the federal probation officer knows about some deal you did, thought of, or talked about, involving a certain amount of marijuana, you'll probably be facing that weight at sentencing.

The general rule is: more dope, more time. The cops, the federal probation officer, and the Assistant United States Attorney seem often to be working to find and/or create scenes and deals just to raise the weight and your time. The poor Placerville, California, marijuana grower with 55 plants never thought it would be so bad until the two cops each counted 55 and then they added them together. The 100-plant magic number appeared and the fun began.

1. Basic Levels for Marijuana and Hash

Level	Pot Weight	Hash Weight	Hash Oil Weight
38	30,000 kg or more	6,000 kg or more	600 kg or more
36	10,000–30,000 kg	2,000–6,000 kg	200–600 kg
34	3,000–10,000 kg	600–2,000 kg	60–200 kg
32	1,000–3,000 kg	200–600 kg	20–60 kg
30	700–1,000 kg	140–200 kg	14–20 kg
28	400–700 kg	80–140 kg	8–14 kg
26	100–400 kg	20–80 kg	2–8 kg
24	80–100 kg	16–20 kg	1.6–2 kg
22	60–80 kg	12–16 kg	1.2–1.6 kg
20	40–60 kg	8–12 kg	800 g–1.2 kg
18	20–40 kg	5–8 kg	500–800 g
16	10–20 kg	2–5 kg	200–500 g
14	5–10 kg	1–2 kg	100–200 g
12	2.5–5 kg	500 g–1 kg	50–100 g
10	1–5 kg	200–500 g	20–50 g
8	250–999 g	50–200 g	5–20 g
6	Less than 250 g	Less than 50 g	Less than 5 g

2. Enhancements

Besides the basic levels for possession, extra points are given for growing on federal property, using booby traps, carrying firearms, playing a leadership role in an organized group, and a myriad of other violations.

The federal laws regarding possession and cultivation of marijuana were last amended in 1995. They are based on the weight of dried, processed marijuana or the number of plants involved in a cultivation.

E. STATUTES AND GUIDELINES

There are two sets of rules that affect federal sentencing. They are the law or statutes and the guidelines. The guidelines are a set of regulations promulgated by the U.S. Sentencing Commission. Despite any guidelines that the Commission makes, federal law takes precedence.

1. Guidelines

a. The guidelines developed by the U.S. Sentencing Commission, and approved by Congress, consider each marijuana plant 100 grams, a little more than 3 1/2 ounces, unless the plant actually weighs more. To find the sentencing level, find the number of plants and move the decimal point one figure to the left. Under these regulations, a person with 99 plants is considered to possess 9.9 kilograms and the offense level is 14. A person with 100 plants is a level 16, and a person with 500 plants is a level 20.

Under federal guidelines, a cutting is considered a plant if it has clearly visible roots. No matter how tiny the plant, whether it is a seedling or a rooted cutting, it is considered 100 grams under the sentencing regulations.

b. Number of Months in Federal Prison

Level	Table 1	Table 2	Table 3	Table 4	Table 5	Table6
6	0–6	1–7	2–8	6–12	9–15	12–19
8	2–8	4–10	6–12	10–15	15–21	18–24
10	6–12	8–14	10–16	15–21	21–27	24–30
12	10–16	12–18	15–21	21–27	27–33	30–37
14	15–21	18–24	21–27	27–33	33–41	37–46
16	21–27	24–30	27–33	33–41	41–51	46–57
18	27–33	30–37	33–41	41–51	51–63	57–71
20	33–41	37–46	41–51	51–60	63–70	70–87
22	41–51	46–57	51–63	63–70	77–96	84–110
24	51–63	57–71	63–78	77–96	92–115	100–137
26	63–78	70–87	78–97	92–115	110–137	120–162
28	78–97	87–108	97–121	110–137	130–162	140–152
30	97–121	108–135	121–151	135–168	151–188	168–210
32	121–151	135–168	151–188	168–210	188–235	210–232
34	151–188	168–210	188–235	210–282	235–293	262–327
36	188–235	210–262	235–290	262–327	292–365	324–405
38	235–283	262–327	282–365	324–405	360–life	360–life

2. Laws

a. Fewer than 50 Kilograms or Plants

The federal law, USC 21 841 1A, states:

> In the case of less than 50 kilograms of marijuana, except in the case of 50 or more marijuana plants regardless of weight or 10 kilograms of hashish or one kilogram of hash oil, such person shall be sentenced to imprisonment for no more than 5 years and a fine of no more than $250,000. If the person has a prior drug conviction, the term of imprisonment shall be no more than 10 years.

This means that if a person has fewer than 50 kilograms or 50 plants they cannot be sentenced to more than 5 years, or 10 years with a previous record. Since the mandatory minimum statutes do not apply, the

Sentencing Commission's regulations are in force. Forty-nine plants is the equivalent of 4.9 kilograms or a level 12, punishable by 10–37 months depending on criminal history. Forty-nine kilograms is a level 20 and is punishable by a sentence of 33–87 months.

b.   Fewer than 100 Kilograms or Plants

This amount falls under the Sentencing Commission's regulations. Each plant is considered 100 grams for sentencing purposes. There is no mandatory sentencing. Ninety-nine plants is the equivalent of 9.9 kilograms and would be a level 14, punishable by 15–46 months. Ninety-nine kilograms is a level 24, punishable by 51–137 months.

c.   100 Plants or Kilograms
USC 21 841 1A states:

> 100 kilograms or more of a mixture containing marijuana or 100 or more marijuana plants regardless of weight. Such a person shall be sentenced to a term of imprisonment not less than 5 years or more than 40. 20 years if death or serious bodily injury occurs, and a fine of up to $2,000,000. With a single prior drug felony: 10 years.

Since the Sentencing Commission considers each plant only 100 grams, a person with 100 plants is a level 16 and is liable only for the mandatory minimum sentence as required by statute. No additional penalties based on weight (unless the actual weight is greater than 100 grams per plant) or plant count would be imposed under Commission regulations. A person caught with nine hundred ninety-nine plants is considered to have only 99 kilograms, and is considered a level 24. With a good record, s/he is liable only for the mandatory minimum sentence as required by statute. Level 24 calls for a 5–40 year sentence. A person with 100–400 kilograms is considered a level 26, subject to 63–162 months.

d.   One Thousand Plants or Kilograms
Another section of the law, Section 841 1A, states:

> Except as otherwise provided in Section 845, 845a, or 845b, any person who violates subsection (a) shall be sentenced as follows:
> 1000 kilograms or more of a mixture or substance containing a detectable amount of marijuana, or 1000 or more marijuana plants regardless of weight:
> Such person shall be sentenced to a term of imprisonment which may not be less than 10 years or more than life and if death or serious bodily injury results from the use of such substance the

term shall not be less than 20 years or more than life, and a fine not to exceed $4,000,000. If a person commits such a violation after a prior conviction of a felony drug offense has become final, the person shall be sentenced to a minimum of 20 years and not more than life and if death or serious bodily injury results from the use of the substance, shall be sentenced to life imprisonment.

This law means that anyone caught with 1,000 plants or 1,000 kilograms is subject to a minimum sentence of 10 years, or 20 years with a prior drug felony. A person with 10,000 plants is considered to have 1,000 kilograms, a level 30, punishable by 97–210 months. A person with 25,000 plants is considered to have 2,500 kilograms, a level 32, punishable by 121–232 months. A person caught with more than 1,500 kilograms is also considered a level 32.

e. Life and Death Penalty

The death penalty for marijuana was enacted in the 1994 crime act. Three different parts of the U.S. Code (USC) affect it. The actual death penalty clause appears in 18USC 3591(D)(b). It states,

> Sentence of Death-A defendant who has been found guilty of an offense referred to in section 848(c)(1), committed as part of a continuing criminal enterprise offense under the conditions described in subsection (b) of that section which involved not less than twice the quantity of controlled substance described in subsection (b)(2)(A) or twice the gross receipts described in (b)(2)(B).

Section 848(c)(1) states,

> (c) For purposes of subsection (a) of this section a person is engaged in a continuing criminal enterprise if-
> (1) he violates any provision of this subchapter or subchapter II of this chapter the punishment for which is a felony, and
> (2) such violation is a part of a continuing series of violations of this subchapter or subchapter II of this chapter-
> (A) which are undertaken by such person in concert with five or more other persons with respect to whom such person occupies a position of organizer, a supervisory position, or any other position of management, and
> (B) from which such person obtains substantial income or resources."

Section 848(b)(2)(A) states,

> Any person who engages in continuing criminal enterprise shall be imprisoned for life and fined in accordance with subsection (a) of this section, if-

(1) such person is the principal administrator, organizer, or leader of the enterprise or is one of several such principal administrators, organizers, or leaders; and

(2)(A) the violation referred to in subsection (c)(1) of this section involved at least 300 times the quantity of a substance described in subsection 841(b)(1)(B) of this title, or

(B) the enterprise, or any other enterprise in which the defendant was the principal or one of several principal administrators, organizers, or leaders received $10 million in gross receipts during any 12 month period of its existence for the manufacture, importation, or distribution of a substance described in section 841(b)(1)(B) of this title.

Section 21 USC 841(b)(1)(B) states,

Except as otherwise provided in section 859, 860 or 861 of this title, any person who violates subsection (a) of this section shall be sentenced as follows:

(vii) 100 kilograms or more of a mixture or substance containing a detectable amount of marijuana or 100 or more marijuana plants regardless of weight.

Section 21 USC 841(b)(1)(B) sets the mandatory sentence for 100 or more marijuana plants. Section 21 USC 848(b)(2)(A) mandates life imprisonment for 300 x 100 plants, or 30,000 plants.

Section 18 USC 3591(b) authorizes the death penalty for "twice the quantity of controlled substance" described in 21 USC 841(b)(1)(B) or a total of 60,000 plants. These plants can be counted cumulatively. For instance, a person with a 3,000 plant indoor garden might harvest four crops a year. In one year s/he would produce 12,000 plants. In five years the garden would produce a total to 60,000 plants.

Another section of the law states,

If a person commits an offense after two or more prior convictions for felony drug offenses have become final, the person shall be sentenced to mandatory life imprisonment.

These laws are in direct violation of the rule of habeas corpus, that the crime with which the defendant is charged must fit the body of evidence. By ascribing an arbitrary set weight to the evidence regardless of its actual weight, the government is discarding one of the major concepts on which our laws have been built and evolved for the past thousand years.

F. THE SAFETY VALVE

The Sentencing Commission enacted a "safety valve" for first time offenders involved in non-violent drug crimes. It was enacted as an emergency amendment effective September 23, 1994, and subsequently approved the following year.

Section 2D1.1(b) is amended by inserting the following subdivision:

If the defendant meets the criteria set forth in subdivisions (1)-(5) of Sec. 5C1.2 (Limitation on Applicability of Statutory Minimum Sentences in Certain Cases) and the offense level determined above is level 26 or greater, decrease by two levels.

The amendments to the 1995 Guidelines Manual states that there are five criteria that defendants must meet to qualify for the reduced sentencing, which is at the judge's discretion. They are:

1.) The defendant has not been previously sentenced to more that six months in prison.

2.) The defendant did not use violence or credible threats of violence or possess a dangerous weapon in connection with the offense.

3.) The offense did not result in death or serious bodily injury to any person.

4.) The defendant was not a leader or organizer of others in the offense and was not engaged in a continuing criminal enterprise.

5.) The defendant truthfully provided all relevant information to the government. (Defendants who do not have any useful information will not be disqualified from the safety valve.)

For example, a defendant convicted of cultivating 150 marijuana plants can escape the five year mandatory minimum sentence and instead be sentenced under the guidelines as if s/he possessed 15 kilograms (150 plants x 100 grams = 15,000 grams), a level 16, yielding a sentence of 21–27 months, rather than the minimum five year sentence.

A person convicted of cultivating 1,500 plants can be sentenced under the guidelines as if s/he possessed 150 kilograms, a level 26 offense. Under section 2D1.1(b)(4) of the guidelines, this person would receive a two-level reduction to a level 24 offense, which yields a sentence of 51–63 months.

G. TIME OFF

Under the federal system, only 15% of the sentence can be subtracted for good behavior. A person sentenced to 10 years in prison serves a minimum of 8½ years.

Drug Policy and Law Resources

Families Against Mandatory Minimums (FAMM)
National Organization working to repeal mandatory sentencing laws.
Website includes resources for people affected by these sentences.
>1612 K Street NW, Suite 1400
>Washington, DC 20006
>Phone: (202) 822-6700
>Website:www.famm.org

Forfeiture Endangers American Rights (FEAR)
Nonprofit organization dedicated to the reform of forfeiture laws.
>Phone: 1-888-FEAR-001
>Website: www.fear.org

The November Coalition
Support organization for prisoners and family members of the War on Drugs.
>795 South Cedar
>Colville, WA 99114
>Website: www.november.org
>Email: moreinfo@november.org

Human Rights 95
Organization dedicated to prisoners' rights and support for casualties of
the War on Drugs
>Website: www.hr95.org

The Lindesmith Center—Drug Policy Foundation
Institutes founded to better inform the public on drug policy and related
issues.
>New York Office
>925 Ninth Avenue
>New York, NY 10019
>Phone: (212) 548-0695

<u>San Francisco Office</u>
2233 Lombard Street
San Francisco, CA 94123
Phone: (415) 921-4987
<u>Office of Legal Affairs</u>
1095 Market Street, Suite 503
San Francisco, CA 94103
Phone: (415) 554-1900
Website: www.lindesmith.org or www.dpf.org

Cannabis Action Network (CAN)
Nonprofit devoted to the reform of all marijuana laws. CAN provides legal referrals, education, activism training, and speakers. Online information clearinghouse.
2560 Bancroft Way #46
Berkeley, CA 94704
Phone: (510) 486-8083
Website: www.cannabisaction.net
Email: mail@cannabisaction.net

Marijuana Policy Project (MPP)
Lobbying organization supporting marijuana law reform.
P.O Box 77492
Capitol Hill
Washington, DC 20013
Phone: (202) 232-5747
Website: www.mpp.org

The Drug Reform Coordination Network (DRCNet)
Organization that directs legislative writing campaigns to change drug laws.
Phone: (202) 293-8340
Website: www.drcnet.org
Email: drcnet@drcnet.org

The Drug Library
The "world's largest online library of drug policy," sponsored by DRCNet.
Website: www.druglibrary.org

Medical Marijuana Resources

Drugsense & The Media Awareness Project

Organizations supporting common-sense solutions and education about the War on Drugs. A resource for links and medical-related information.

P.O. Box 651 Porterville, CA 93258

Phone: 1-800-266-5759

Website: www.drugsense.org

www.mapinc.org

Multidisciplinary Association for Psychedelic Studies (MAPS)

Organization dedicated to medical research involving psychedelics and to changing public policy concerning drugs.

2105 Robinson Ave.

Sarasota, FL 34232

Phone: (941) 924-6277

Website: www.maps.org

Alliance for Cannabis Therapeutics

Information about medical uses of cannabis including legal links, policy information, and scientific study results.

Website: marijuana-as-medicine.org/alliance.htm

Quick Trading Company

Parent company to the publisher of this book and patient rights activists. Information provider to the medical marijuana cause.

Website: www.quicktrading.com

Email: fredquick@quicktrading.com

The Cannabis Information Network

Informational online site dedicated to marijuana and hemp.
  Website: www.marijuana-hemp.com

The International Cannabinoid Research Society (ICRS)

Nonprofit organization dedicated to research in all cannabinoid related fields, from receptor studies and medicinal chemistry to treatment and prevention of marijuana abuse.
  55 Elsom Pkwy.
  S. Burlington, VT 05403
  Phone: (802) 865-0970
  Website: CannabinoidSociety.org
  Email: ICRS@together.net

INDEX

A

accidents
  and drug busts, 2
  and drug testing, 115
  preventing, 8, 12
activism, 171–74
ADA. *See* American Disabilities Act
adulterants, 128, 131–32
aerial surveillance, 19–22, 31–32
affidavits, 6, 36, 48
American Disabilities Act, 112
appearance. *See* suspicious activity and
  standing out
arraignment, 54
arrest record. *See* record, arrest
arrests, 49, 66, 73
  citizen, 66, 73
  v. detention, 28, 72
See also post-arrest; questioning; resisting
  arrest; rights, arrestee's; warrants
arrest warrant. *See* warrants, arrest
Ask Ed questions, 6, 8,16–17, 18, 20–21,
  24–25, 31, 34, 38, 44–46, 57, 70, 77
attorneys. *See* lawyers; public defenders
automobiles
  and drug busts, 8–11, 15
  license plates, 29
See also penalties; searches, auto

B

bail, 48–50, 54
bias in drug tests, 124–25, 127, 141
Bill of Rights, 53, 160–61
See also Constitution, U.S.
blood tests. *See* drug tests, blood
business records, as evidence.
  See evidence, records as

C

cannabis. *See* marijuana; medical
  marijuana
caregivers and medical marijuana, 94, 96,
  99, 100
cars. *See* automobiles
cash as evidence. *See* evidence, money as;
  suspicious activity, wealth as
cell phones. *See* phones
charges, 71
  civil v. criminal, 160
  reduction of, 2, 3, 30
See also felonies; hearings, preliminary;
  infractions; misdemeanors; penalties
chelating agents, 129, 131
citizen arrests. *See* arrests, citizen
citizen informers. *See* informers, citizen
clean-up after arrest. *See* post-arrest
client control, 160
clothing as evidence. *See* evidence,
  clothing as
confirmation tests, 112, 121–23
See also gas chromatography/mass
  spectrometry test
Constitution, U.S., 30, 46, 53, 61, 111,
  136–38, 160–61
continuing criminal enterprise, 25,
  168–70
cops. *See* police
courtroom defense preparation, 13, 15,
  55, 61, 81–82, 162
  medical, 35, 57, 97. *See also* medical
   necessity
cultivation. *See* penalties; reduction of
  risk as a grower
curtilage, 62–63
cutoff levels, 123, 127, 134

D

DATIA. *See* Drug and Alcohol Testing Industry Association
DEA. *See* Drug Enforcement Agency
death penalty, 168
See also penalties
defense strategies. *See* courtroom defense preparation
delivery services. *See* mail delivery services
detection. *See* aerial surveillance; infrared technologies
detection time for marijuana, 112, 123, 125–28
detention, 49, 66, 68–69, 72
  v. arrest, 28, 44, 72
discussing use as evidence. *See* reduction of risk through discretion
doctor, finding a marijuana-friendly, 100–102
See also medical recommendation for marijuana use
doctor–patient relationship, 93, 98–100
documentation
  of drug test, 135–36
  of medical use, 100, 105. *See also* court defense preparation, medical
  of search and seizure, 50, 52, 56
See also evidence, records as; reduction of risk through preplanning
driver's license suspension. *See* penalties
Drug and Alcohol Testing Industry Association (DATIA), 108, 140–41
drug busts. *See* accidents and drug busts; automobiles and drug busts; searches; suspicious activity; warrants
Drug Enforcement Agency (DEA), 37–39
Drug Free Workplace Act, 109
drug reform organizations.
  See organizations, drug reform
drug testing legislation, 109, 111–17, 119–21, 130, 132–33, 137, 140–41
drug tests
  blood, 118, 125

  challenging results to, 134–36, 138–39
  hair, 118, 123–25
  passing, 127–33
  performance times, 113–15
  perspiration, 119, 126–27
  and private v. public employees, 108, 110–11, 115, 117, 135
  saliva, 119, 125–26
  urine, 116, 118–23, 136, 138
See also evidence, physical; false positive on drug test; random drug testing; rights, employee
Drug War. *See* War on Drugs

E

electricity
  increased use as evidence, 5, 20, 21, 29, 30
  stealing, 16, 17
  tampering with, 9
emergencies. *See* exigent circumstances
evidence, 54, 55, 58
  clothing as, 19, 22, 23
  garbage as, 27
  garden tools as, 23, 26, 27
  money as, 4, 23, 37, 39, 50–51
  packaging supplies as, 11, 12, 23, 42, 51, 55
  photos as, 24–25
  physical, 69–70
  records as, 5, 23, 24, 35, 36, 39, 42, 51
  seizure of, 24–25, 46
  See also seizures
  suppression of, 42, 60–61, 63–64, 162
  testimony as, 4, 163–164
  See also informers
exigent circumstances, 9, 44–46, 60, 66

F

false positive on drug test, 133–34
Families Against Mandatory Minimums (FAMM), 77, 171

See also mandatory minimum sentences
federal drug testing guidelines. *See* drug testing legislation
federal sentencing guidelines, 3, 70, 162–67, 170
  and sentencing levels, 163–167
fees, legal. *See* lawyers and fees
felonies, 48, 54–55, 67, 71, 73
fences, 21, 23, 30, 61, 63
See also curtilage
fire. *See* exigent circumstances
firearms. *See* guns
FLIR (Forward-looking infrared radar). *See* infrared technology
forfeiture, 50, 52, 56–57
Fourth Amendment, 30, 46, 160
  and drug tests, 111, 136, 138
See also searches, drug tests as

G

garbage
  as evidence, 27
  at grow site, 17, 19, 20
  searches, 5
gardens
  general precautions, 26, 57–58
  outdoor, 17, 19–23
garden supply stores
  as informers, 6, 36
  surveilled, 37–38
garden tools as evidence. *See* evidence, garden tools as
gas chromatography/mass spectrometry test, 120–24, 131, 133, 134
See also confirmation tests; drug tests; immunoassay drug tests
grower precautions. *See* reduction of risk as a grower
guns, 23, 25, 39, 47, 103, 165, 170

H

habeas corpus, 169
hearings
  bail, 48–49
  preliminary, 54–55
See also courtroom defense preparation; felonies

I

immunoassay drug tests, 120–24, 131, 133, 134
See also drug tests; gas chromatography/mass spectrometry test
imprisonment. *See* penalties
incarceration. *See* penalties
informers, 2–4, 7, 28, 29, 31, 33
  anonymous, 15, 30
  citizen, 5, 6, 30
  incentives for, 2, 3, 5, 25
  recognizing, 3, 4
  replying to, 6
  robbers as, 6
See also garden supply stores; mail delivery services; neighbor relations; privacy, right to
infractions, 71
infrared technology, 5, 22, 30, 31
insurance plans, legal, 78

L

law, federal v. state, 161–62. *See also* drug testing legislation; penalties
lawyers
  and bail, 48, 49, 69
  changing, 88–89
  choosing, 57, 76–83
  and client control, 90
  and fees, 84–85
  licenses, 76
  misrepresentation by, 87–88
  relationship w/ client, 82–84, 86, 89–90
  retainers, 84
See also courtroom defense preparation; hearings, preliminary; questioning, right to a lawyer's presence at
legal insurance plans. *See* insurance plans, legal

legal referral programs *See* programs, legal referral
legal resources, 171–72
loose talk. *See* reducing risk through discretion

M

mail delivery services, 5, 36–37, 162
See also penalties
mail order
  books, 38
  seeds, 38
  supplies, 37
mandatory minimum sentences, 70, 77, 143–44, 146–50, 152–58, 161, 163, 166–67, 169–70
See also penalties
marijuana
  color and detection, 22, 30
  decriminalization, 151
  quantity, 35–35, 49, 55, 57, 70, 161, 163–70
  as schedule I drug, 93
  smell, 44–45
  statistics. *See* statistics
  tourism, viii
  transporting, 8
See also medical marijuana; penalties
Marinol®, 101
  and drug tests, 134
medical marijuana
  doctor–patient relationship, 93, 98–100
  and medical conditions, 97–99
  quantity, 92, 94, 100, 103
  registries, 92, 93, 98, 103–4
  resources, 173–74
  state laws, 92–101, 104, 106, 145–46
medical necessity, 95, 96, 97, 104
See also courtroom defense preparation, medical
medical recommendation for marijuana use, 96–97, 102, 105
See also doctor, finding a marijuana-friendly
minors, rights of, 29, 43
Miranda rights, 47, 67–68
misdemeanors, 57, 67, 71, 73
money as evidence. *See* evidence, money as; suspicious activity, wealth as

N

narcs. *See* informers
neighbor relations, 3, 29, 30, 33, 45
NIDA-5, 112–13, 119, 126
no contest plea, 72
noncitizens, precautions for, 11, 70

O

Omnibus Transportation Employee Testing Act, 109
open fields doctrine, 62
organizations, drug reform, 77, 171–72
See also programs
outdoor garden. *See* gardens, outdoor
ownership v. possession, 12–14, 16

P

paraphernalia, 34
See also penalties
paths, in grow area. *See* gardens, outdoors
penalties, 143–58, 166–70
  federal, 144
  federal v. state, 143
  reduction of, 170
  state by state, 144–58
  for subsequent offenses, 144–45, 147–58, 169
personal use, marijuana for. *See* possession
phones
  post-arrest calls, 69–70
  and privacy, 26
See also wiretaps
photographs
  developing, 24
  of house after search, 50

incriminating, 24, 25
pipes. *See* paraphernalia
plain view, 12, 44–47
plants, marijuana. *See* marijuana
police
    conduct, 32, 34, 43, 45, 47, 49, 53,
        60, 67–68
    replying to, 13–16, 28, 29, 42, 47, 53,
        67, 104–6
    undercover, 4, 7, 15, 28, 33, 45
police searches. *See* searches
possession, 15, 43, 63–64, 71, 143
    v. ownership, 12–14, 16
    v. sale/distribution, 143
    See also penalties
post-arrest, 50–51, 69–70
    See also bail; hearings; lawyers
power usage. *See* electricity
precautions, *See* noncitizens, precautions
    for; reduction of risk
preliminary hearings. *See* hearings,
    preliminary
privacy
    in automobile, 11,14
    and ownership, 12, 13
    and property, 27. *See also* curtilage
    right to, 43, 61, 64, 83, 103, 138
    See also plain view
probable cause, 43, 45, 55, 64, 73,
    113, 138
    See also Fourth Amendment
programs
    diversion, 54
    legal referral, 76–77
property issues. *See* curtilage; forfeiture;
    privacy
public defenders, 85–89
    changing, 88–89
    helping, 89
    See also lawyers

Q

questioning, right to a lawyer's presence
    at, 47, 53, 67, 68

R

random drug testing, 115, 138
    See also drug tests
record keeping. *See* documentation;
    evidence, records as; photos;
    reduction of risk through
        preplanning
    recourse for drug test results, 134–137
reduction of charges. *See* charges,
    reduction of
reduction of risk, x–xi, 17, 29, 82–83
    in automobile, 10–12
    through discretion, 3, 8–10, 24, 32,
        33, 135, 163
    as a grower, 8, 17, 19, 21, 22, 24, 26,
        32, 34–37, 57–58
    through preplanning, 13, 29, 48, 56
    See also photos; police, replying to;
        suspicious activity
reform organizations, 77, 171–74
replying to police. *See* police,
    replying to
resisting arrest, 67
rights
    arrestee, 54, 67–68, 70, 72
    See also post-arrest
    civil, 110, 137
    employee, 138
    See also Bill of Rights; Miranda rights;
        privacy, right to
    right to remain silent, 13, 16, 28, 29, 47,
        53, 67
    See also Miranda rights
rip-offs. *See* theft
risk reduction. *See* reduction of risk

S

safety valve, 170
sale. *See* penalties
scientific process of drug tests, 118,
    120–21
    See also drug tests; immunoassay drug
        tests; gas chromatography/ mass
        spectrometry test

searches, 60
  of automobile, 10, 11
  and consent, 12–14, 28, 43
  drug test as, 136
  illegal, 30, 55, 60, 64
  scope of, 44, 46, 60
  with warrant, 28, 47
  without warrant, 42–45
  See also curtilage; Fourth Amendment;
    privacy; warrants
  search warrants. *See* warrants
seizure, 22, 52, 63–64
  of evidence, 24–25, 46
  of property, 52, 56
  See also forfeiture; Fourth Amendment
sentencing
  and guns, 23
  and offense level, 163
  reduction of, 170
  See also federal sentencing guidelines,
    penalties
snitches. *See* informers
standing, 63–64
  See also suppression of evidence
statistics
  on drug testing, 108, 110, 112, 139,
    140, 141
  on marijuana arrests, ix, xi–xii
  on marijuana use, ix, xii
statute of limitations, 66
  See also warrants, arrest
stupid grower tricks, 8
  See also reduction of risk
substitution of urine sample, 131
  See also drug tests
surveillance, aerial. *See* aerial
  surveillance; infrared technologies
suspicious activity, 10
  and drug busts, 2, 21, 42, 62
  and standing out, 15, 17–19, 32–33
  wealth as, 9, 10
  See also automobiles; neighbor relations;
    reduction of risk

T

testing. *See* drug tests; evidence, physical
theft, 5, 16, 22, 35, 38, 39
  by police, 7, 51–52
thermal imaging, 30–31
  See also infrared technologies
trash. *See* garbage
trespassing. *See* curtilage; privacy

U

undercover police. *See* police, undercover
United States Constitution. *See*
  Constitution, U.S.
urine tests. *See* drug tests, urine
U.S. sentencing guidelines. *See* federal
  sentencing guidelines

V

violence, 23, 39, 170
  as part of offense, 163

W

War on Drugs, ix, xi, xii, 4, 7, 108–9,
  140–41
warrants
  arrest, 66–67, 73
  from informer tip, 5
  for phone tap, 26
  search, 5, 29, 33, 36, 38, 42–47, 55,
    62, 64, 162
  traffic, 67
  See also searches
water
  leaks, 9
  lines and detection, 22
weight conversions, English to metric, 143
wiretaps, 26
workplace and drug testing. *See* drug
  tests; rights, employee

Z

zero tolerance, 57